iPhoto® for iPad®

Richard Wentk

SUR
COUNTY

WILEY

Wiley Publishing, Inc.

Teach Yourself VISUALLY™ iPhoto® for iPad®

Published by
John Wiley & Sons, Inc.
10475 Crosspoint Boulevard
Indianapolis, IN 46256

www.wiley.com

Published simultaneously in Canada

Wiley publishes in a variety of print and electronic formats and by print-on-demand. Some material included with standard print versions of this book may not be included in e-books or in print-on-demand. If this book refers to media such as a CD or DVD that is not included in the version you purchased, you may download this material at http://booksupport.wiley.com. For more information about Wiley products, visit www.wiley.com.

Library of Congress Control Number: 2013934421

ISBN: 978-1-118-44360-6

Manufactured in the United States of America

10 9 8 7 6 5 4 3 2 1

Trademark Acknowledgments

Contact Us

For general information on our other products and services please contact our Customer Care Department within the U.S. at 877-762-2974, outside the U.S. at 317-572-3993 or fax 317-572-4002.

For technical support please visit www.wiley.com/techsupport.

WILEY Sales | Contact Wiley at (877) 762-2974 or fax (317) 572-4002.

Credits

Acquisitions Editor
Aaron Black

Sr. Project Editor
Sarah Hellert

Technical Editor
Dennis R. Cohen

Copy Editor
Scott Tullis

Editorial Director
Robyn Siesky

Business Manager
Amy Knies

Sr. Marketing Manager
Sandy Smith

Vice President and Executive Group Publisher
Richard Swadley

Vice President and Executive Publisher
Barry Pruett

Project Coordinator
Patrick Redmond

Graphics and Production Specialists
Ronda David-Burroughs
Jennifer Goldsmith
Jennifer Mayberry

Proofreader
Sossity R. Smith

Indexer
BIM Indexing & Proofreading Services

About the Author

Richard Wentk has been writing professionally about technology and creativity since 1993. He is a regular contributor to numerous magazines including the *British Journal of Photography, Total Digital Photography, Digital Camera,* and *Computer Arts*. He is an Associate Member of the Royal Photographic Society and exhibits work regularly in the United Kingdom. He is also an app developer and the author of a number of books for developers and Mac users including the *iOS App Development Portable Genius*. For the latest news and information, visit his site at www. zettaboom.com.

Author's Acknowledgments

All books are a collaboration, and this one is no exception. I'd like to thank Aaron Black for giving the green light to this project and Sarah Hellert for making the transition from copy to printed item as painless as possible.
Special thanks are due to Hans Peter Blochwitz, Jos van Galen, Rhys Jones, and Justyna Furmanczyk for permission to use their superb photos.
Extra special thanks to Annette Saunders for contributing further exemplary photos and for making the writing process far more pleasurable than it would have been otherwise.

How to Use This Book

Who This Book Is For

This book is for the reader who has never used this particular technology or software application. It is also for readers who want to expand their knowledge.

The Conventions in This Book

1 Steps

This book uses a step-by-step format to guide you easily through each task. **Numbered steps** are actions you must do; **bulleted steps** clarify a point, step, or optional feature; and **indented steps** give you the result.

2 Notes

Notes give additional information — special conditions that may occur during an operation, a situation that you want to avoid, or a cross-reference to a related area of the book.

3 Icons and Buttons

Icons and buttons show you exactly what you need to click to perform a step.

4 Tips

Tips offer additional information, including warnings and shortcuts.

5 Bold

Bold type shows command names or options that you must click or text or numbers you must type.

6 Italics

Italic type introduces and defines a new term.

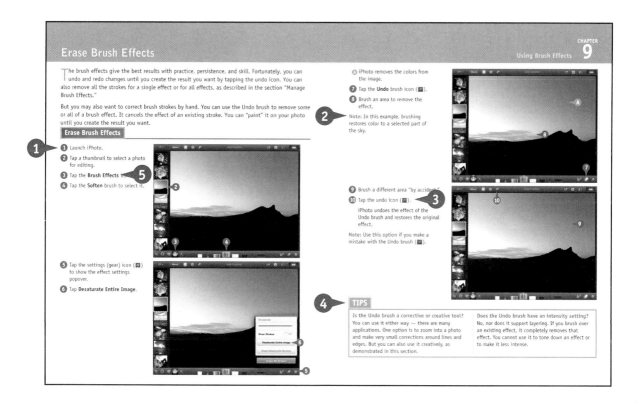

Table of Contents

Chapter 3 Using iCloud and Photo Stream

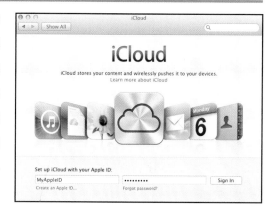

Chapter 4 Introducing Photo Browsing

Table of Contents

Chapter 8   Correcting and Enhancing Photos

Chapter 9   Using Brush Effects

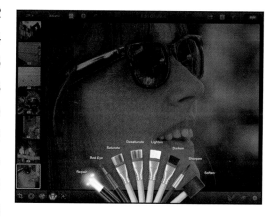

Table of Contents

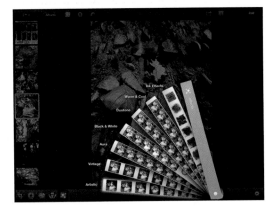

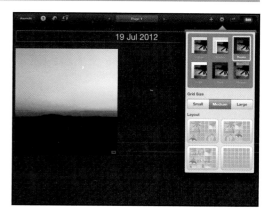

CHAPTER 1

Discovering iPhoto for iOS

iPhoto for iOS offers many great features for editing, organizing, sharing, and displaying photos. In this chapter you learn the basics of iPhoto and discover how to get started with photos, albums, events, and journals on the iPad and iPhone.

Take a First Look at iPhoto

iPhoto is designed to help you get more from your photography. But before you can begin editing and sharing your photos, you must understand how iPhoto groups your photos into collections.

You can use iPhoto as a stand-alone app, but iPhoto works closely with other apps: Camera and Photo on iOS devices, and iTunes and iPhoto on the Mac. Supporting iPhoto with these other applications helps you get the most from iPhoto by keeping your photos organized and ready to share.

Understanding iPhoto Browsing

iPhoto can display all the photos in your device in a single list. This option can be spectacular, but it can also be difficult to search for a specific photo. To help you find photos, iPhoto can group related photos into collections. The three collection types appear on the main iPhoto launch page: Albums, Events, and Journals. Each has its quirks. Some features may not work as you expect.

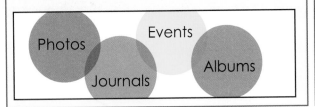

Understanding Albums

iPhoto displays three kinds of albums. You can group any of your photos into a named album using the Photos app on an iOS device. You can also create albums using iPhoto on the Mac, and import them to your device through iTunes or by uploading them to Apple's Photo Stream service. iPhoto for iOS creates albums automatically when you select photos as favorites, when you edit photos, or when you *beam* photos between devices by sharing them over Wi-Fi. You can also tag photos with your own keywords. iPhoto automatically creates *tag albums* for photos that share a tag.

Understanding Events

Events organize your photos by date. You can import events from your Mac iPhoto library using iTunes. This is a good way to display your existing photo collections. Events are also created automatically when you import photos from a digital camera or memory card using the iPad Camera Connection Kit. You cannot create events any other way.

Understanding Journals

You can use journals to display your photos in a beautiful layout with supporting text, maps, calendar dates, and other details. Journals are for sharing, not for browsing. You can upload them to your iCloud account as a web page and send the link to friends and family.

June 13 - I met this stern-looking fellow this morning as I came out of my tent. He just stared at me with an affronted air, as if he couldn't quite place who I was and

June 14 - I saw this beautiful bird. It only stayed briefly; though I kept quite still and very quiet, it decided something was not quite right about me, and flew off.

Browse Groups of Photos

You can use the buttons on the main iPhoto launch screen to browse photos and view your albums, events, and journals.

You can also swap between the different views by swiping left or right at the top or bottom of the screen.

Ⓐ Help Button

Displays the iPhoto help pages.

Ⓑ Albums Button

Displays a list of albums on your device.

Ⓒ Photos Button

Displays every photo on your device without trying to group them.

Ⓓ Events Button

Shows a list of events on your device.

Ⓔ Journals Button

Displays the journals you have created.

View Photos

When you first fire up iPhoto and tap the Photos button on the launch page, iPhoto shows you every photo stored on your device as a list of *thumbnails* — small preview images.

To browse your photos, scroll through the list. A Power Scroll feature at the right of the window makes it easy to scroll through them quickly. iPhoto displays the month and date of the photos as you scroll through them.

View Photos

① Tap the **iPhoto** icon on the Home screen to launch iPhoto.

Note: If you use iPhoto regularly, you can tap and hold its icon to rearrange your app display and drag the iPhoto icon to the Dock for quick access.

iPhoto launches.

② If the thumbnails do not appear, tap the **Photos** button.

The list of thumbnails appears.

③ Drag your finger up and down on the Power Scroll bar to move quickly through the photos.

Ⓐ iPhoto displays the month and date as you scroll.

Note: To scroll more slowly, drag your finger on the photo grid.

④ Tap any photo to view it.

iPhoto displays the photo in an Editor screen with a selection of editing controls and a smaller thumbnails list.

⑤ Tap the **Photos** button to return to the list of albums.

Note: You can swipe your finger left and right in the Editor to view further photos.

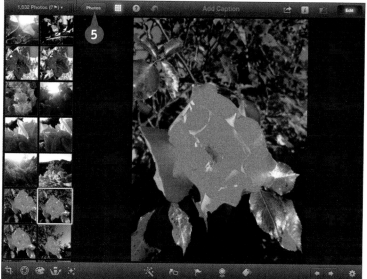

TIPS

Is there a quick way to scroll to the top of the thumbnails?

Tap the status bar on your device — the area at the top of the screen that displays the time, battery charge, Wi-Fi signal strength, and other status information. iPhoto quickly scrolls to the top of the thumbnails list. Unfortunately there is no quick way to scroll to the end of the list.

Can I view the list in portrait mode?

In portrait mode, the display shows slightly more photos per screen than in landscape mode. To select portrait mode, rotate the device to one of the two possible portrait orientations with the home button and connector port at the top or bottom. The thumbnail display rotates automatically.

Explore Albums

You can view the albums on your device by tapping the Albums button on the iPhoto start page. The albums feature displays the albums you create in iPhoto for the Mac, Photoshop Elements, Aperture, or the iOS Photos app. You can create *tag albums* by adding tag keywords to a photo, as described in Chapter 6. You cannot create standard albums.

iPhoto maintains a collection of special albums for your convenience, including edited photos and photos you mark with the flag and favorite (rosette) symbols. The iOS camera roll and photos you beam — wirelessly import — from other devices also appear in special albums.

Explore Albums

1. Launch iPhoto.

2. If the Albums page does not appear, tap the **Albums** button.

iPhoto displays a list of albums.

Note: The Edited, Flagged, Beamed, and Favorites albums appear only after you edit, beam, flag, or favorite a photo.

Note: Named albums appear only if you create them in the Photos app or import them via iTunes or Photo Stream.

3. If there are more than 12 albums, drag your finger up and down to scroll through the list.

4. Tap any album to view it.

iPhoto displays the photos in the album in the small thumbnails list at one side of the screen and loads the first photo in the Editor.

5 Swipe left or right to view further photos in the album.

Note: You can also view photos by tapping them in the thumbnails list.

6 Tap the **Albums** button to return to the main thumbnails list.

TIPS

Why do albums appear in different colors?
The colors help you recognize the different types of albums. The albums you create yourself appear with a gray border. The Camera Roll album appears with a gray-blue border. The remaining albums are generated and maintained by iPhoto. They appear with a light brown border.

What is the Photo Box album?
There is no way to delete a photo permanently in iPhoto. If you use the Photos app to delete a photo from your device after you edit it, select it as a favorite, or use it in a journal, iPhoto keeps a copy of the photo in the Edited album. If you then remove the photo's edits or tags or remove it from a journal, iPhoto moves it to Photo Box — because it has nowhere else to put it.

View Events

Events are groups of photos arranged by date. iPhoto automatically splits photos into events when you import them from a digital camera or SD card using the iPad Camera Connection Kit. You can view events on your device by tapping the Events button on the iPhoto start page.

You can also import events from iPhoto on the Mac using iTunes or Photo Stream. This is a good way to set up an iPad as a portable photo album. There is no way to create events in iPhoto itself.

View Events

1 Launch iPhoto.

2 If the Events page does not appear, tap the **Events** button.

iPhoto displays a list of events.

Note: If there are no events, the page displays a note about importing and creating them.

3 If there are more than 12 events, drag your finger up and down to scroll through the list.

4 Tap any event to view it.

iPhoto displays the photos in the event in the small thumbnails list at one side of the screen and also loads the first photo into the Editor.

⑤ Swipe left or right to view further photos in the event.

Note: You can also view photos by tapping them in the thumbnails list.

⑥ Tap the **Events** button to return to the main thumbnails list.

TIPS

Why do some thumbnails include small white icons?
If you edit, flag, or favorite a photo, iPhoto adds a matching small icon to it to remind you — for example, flagged photos show a small flag. The icons appear in the thumbnails when you view events and albums, but not in the main photo list.

Can I rearrange the order of events?
Events are listed in date order, so you cannot rearrange them. However, you can create and rearrange events in iPhoto for the Mac and download them into iPhoto for iOS. This is a very indirect way to change the order, but it does work.

Explore Journals

You can use journals to collect related photos and display them as web pages with additional comments, date icons, map locations, and other information.

Journals are designed to be shared. You can upload them to iCloud and share them as web links. You can also view them on a device. In iPhoto, collecting photos in a journal, tapping them to open them, and swiping through them is the only way to view them full screen.

Explore Journals

1 Launch iPhoto.

2 If the Journals page does not appear, tap the **Journals** button.

The list of journals appears.

Note: If you have not created any journals, this page displays a brief note about creating them.

3 Tap any journal to view its contents.

Note: You can read more about creating and editing journals in Chapter 13.

iPhoto displays the contents of the journal.

Ⓐ Optionally, tap any photo to view it full screen.

Note: You can swipe through the photos in the journal in full-screen mode.

④ Tap the **Journals** button to return to the list of journals.

⑤ Tap the **Edit** button to enter edit mode.

iPhoto adds two icons to each journal so you can delete or favorite the journals in the list.

⑥ Tap the delete icon (⊗) of any journal to delete it.

⑦ Tap the favorite (rosette) icon (◉) of any journal to mark it as a favorite.

iPhoto adds a small white favorite symbol to the journal.

⑧ Tap the **Edit** button again to leave edit mode.

TIPS

Why would I use journals instead of albums or events?
Albums are a collection of photos. Journals are a collection of photos laid out on pages with supporting text, notes, titles, dates, map locations, and other supporting information. You cannot create albums or events in iPhoto, but you can create journals.

Do I need an iCloud account to use journals?
You can create and view journals on your device without an iCloud account and without Internet access. iCloud is essential only if you want to share your journals with friends, family, and colleagues online.

Investigate iPhoto Settings

Like most apps, iPhoto includes a selection of preferences and settings. You can use the settings to make minor changes to iPhoto's features.

None of the settings are critically important, and you can use iPhoto without modifying them. But you can get more from iPhoto if you understand what the settings do and know how to find them.

Investigate iPhoto Settings

1 Launch iPhoto.

2 Tap any of the following buttons: **Albums**, **Photos**, **Events**, or **Journals**.

3 Tap the settings (gear) icon (✷) to display the settings popover.

iPhoto displays a popover with a selection of settings.

4 Turn on the **Wireless Beaming** switch to allow other devices to send photos wirelessly to your device.

5 Turn on the **Include Photo Location** and **Location Lookup** switches to allow iPhoto to embed location information in photos and journals.

6 Turn on the **Sound Effects** switch to play sounds as you use iPhoto.

7 Turn on **Mirror on TV** to show the iPhoto interface when you view photos on a connected TV or monitor.

8 Tap anywhere on the screen outside the popover to close it and save your changes.

TIPS

Does iPhoto have any other preferences?
You can access the preferences of many iOS apps by tapping the settings (gear) icon (✿) on the home page and tapping the icon of the app in the list that appears. iPhoto uses this feature to display a version number, acknowledgements, and legal information, but you cannot use it to change any further preferences.

Why would I turn off photo location sharing?
If you take photos at home and include location information when you share them, anyone can find your address from the photo. This can be very bad for your privacy and security. Always share personal photos with location information turned off.

Get Help

iPhoto includes built-in help. You can access the help from any page in iPhoto to learn more about the features on that page. You can also browse through the help pages to learn more about all of iPhoto's features.

To access the help pages, tap the help icon. On the albums, photos, events, and journals pages the icon displays the main help file for browsing. On any Editor page, the icon displays help tips for that page.

Get Help

1 Launch iPhoto.

2 Tap any of the following buttons: **Albums**, **Photos**, **Events**, or **Journals**.

3 Tap the help icon (⊙) at the top left of the page.

iPhoto displays a popover with a selection of help headings.

4 Tap any heading in the list to view the help for a topic.

Note: You can browse through the help topics by tapping the name and using the navigation button at the top left of the help popover to return when done.

5 Tap **Done** when finished.

iPhoto hides the popover.

Note: You cannot hide the help popover by tapping outside it.

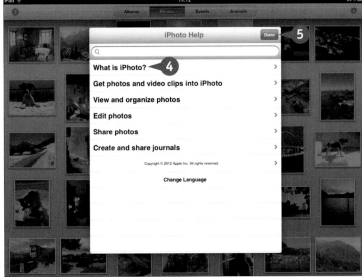

6 Tap any event or album to open an Editor page.

7 Tap the help icon (🕐) to view help notes for the page.

In the Editor pages only, iPhoto overlays help notes for each unique feature on the page.

8 Read a help note to see a quick tip for each feature.

9 Tap the arrow (▶) next to a note to view more detailed help.

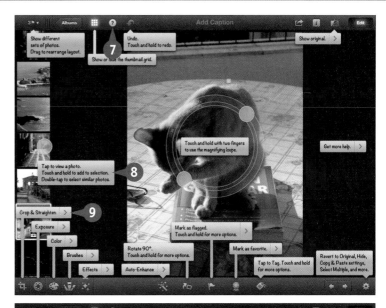

iPhoto displays the relevant help page in the main help document.

10 Tap **Done** when finished.

A Optionally, tap the top left navigation button to browse other help topics.

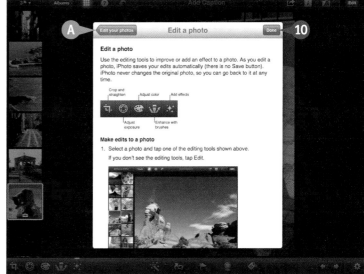

TIPS

Why are some help tips missing?
iPhoto does not repeat help notes. If an icon has no help note, it is described on some other page. In the Editor, go up a level using the top left navigation button and try tapping the help icon (🕐) on that page instead.

iPhoto is easy to use. Do I need to read the help?
iPhoto has many hidden features. Even if you find iPhoto easy to use, you can find many useful hints and tips in the help.

Find Further Help Online

Although the built-in help is detailed and comprehensive, you may have further questions about iPhoto. You can use the Apple Support Forums to get help for specific questions.

The support forums are free and easy to search. You may find that other users have already asked and answered your question. You can also use the rest of the Internet to search for help.

Find Further Help Online

1 Launch any web browser.

2 Type **http://discussions. apple.com** into the address bar.

Note: Do not type the /index. jspa suffix — it appears automatically when the page loads.

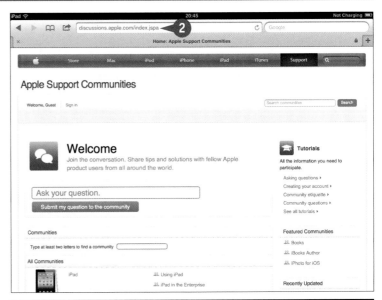

The browser displays the Apple Support Communities page.

3 Scroll down the list to find the iOS Apps heading.

4 Click or tap the **iPhoto for iOS** link on the page.

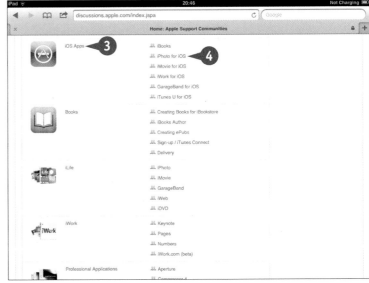

The browser displays questions and answers about iPhoto for iOS.

⑤ Tap any category to view relevant questions and answers.

⑥ Optionally, scroll down to read the most recent discussions.

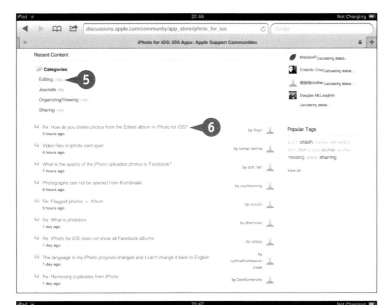

⑦ Scroll to the top of the page when done.

⑧ Type a question to search all support discussions for related words.

Note: If you register on the forums, you can start your own question topics.

TIPS

Why do some of the answers apply to iPhoto for Mac?

Even if you search on the iPhoto for iOS discussion page, the search returns answers for related software, included iPhoto for the Mac. There is no way to limit answers to iPhoto for iOS at this time.

Can I find other help online?

You can use any search engine to find tips and answers to questions. Most searches return answers to questions about iPhoto for the Mac. You can avoid this by including "iOS," "iPad," or "iPhone" in your search question.

Investigate Other Apps

You can use other apps from the App Store to expand your creative options. Competing apps offer extra features and have different strengths. They do not integrate quite so seamlessly with other Apple applications, but it is easy to share photos between apps, and to use the features of one app to supplement the features of the others. All apps work with the camera roll, and some also work with albums and events.

Apps are cheap. You can buy a collection of powerful apps for much less than the cost of a single desktop photo editing application.

PS Express

Photoshop Express is free. You can use it for very basic editing, including cropping, rotation, and image flipping. You can also apply borders, tints, and other visual effects. But you cannot copy and paste images, adjust the color balance, or zoom into part of a photo. Digital noise reduction, which can help eliminate graininess from photos shot in poor light, is available as a $3.99 add-on. At the time of writing, Photoshop Express does not work with the iPad 2 camera.

PS Touch

Photoshop Touch ($9.99) includes many of the powerful features in the desktop version of Photoshop Elements, including cropping, color, contrast and exposure control, rotation, and a good selection of preset filters. You can select an area for editing using your fingers. You can also blend multiple photos and selections together. Because Photoshop Touch is so powerful, it requires an iPad 2 or later, running iOS 5 or later.

Instagram

You can use Instagram to apply simple filters and effects to photos and share them to the most popular social networking sites, including Facebook, Twitter, Flickr, Tumblr, Foursquare, and Posterous. The effects are limited but easy to use. Instagram has become very popular because its users can create photos with a strong mood and feel and share them with their friends and social followers almost instantly. The app is free and runs on the iPad as an emulated iPhone app.

Snapseed

Chosen as Apple's own App of the Year in 2011, Snapseed ($4.99) is a popular and powerful editor. Built-in help makes the app very intuitive. You can use the filters to add moods and textures to your photos, with adjustable controls. Snapseed falls midway between the one-touch effects of Instagram and the more complex editing available in Photoshop Touch. The editing options are limited compared to a desktop photo editor, but you can get attractive results very quickly.

App Store › Photo & Video › Nik Software, Inc.

Snapseed
Description

** Best Mobile Photo App 2012 ** (TIPA)
** iPad App of the Year!** …

Nik Software, Inc. Web Site ›   Snapseed Support ›

Downloaded ▾   What's New in Version 1.4

Luminance

Luminance ($0.99) is a popular photo editor with limited features and good social sharing options. You can crop photos, or adjust the color and contrast. You can also apply a limited selection of preset color effects, and create your own presets. The design makes it easy to apply multiple effects at the same time. Some users may find it simpler to work with than iPhoto's more complex adjustment options, but Luminance lacks iPhoto's brush-based editing.

App Store › Photo & Video › Subsplash

Luminance
Description

Luminance gives you pro photo editing capabilities in a simp
want, and copy edits you've made from one photo and apply

Subsplash Web Site ›   Luminance Support ›

Downloaded ▾   What's New in Version 1.2

Pixlr-o-matic

Pixlr-o-matic is another package of preset filters. The design is attractive, but the features are limited to preset effects that you have no control over. Social sharing is simple and built-in. The basic version of the app is free. The plus version ($0.99) adds in-app purchase of further preset filter packs. The app competes with Instagram and is worth considering for mood and atmosphere, but it does not compete with iPhoto as a serious editing tool.

App Store › Photo & Video › Autodesk Inc.

Pixlr-o-matic
Description

Don't miss one of the most talked about and popular photo a
stunning shots.
This fun and simple darkroom app makes it easy to add an e

Autodesk Inc. Web Site ›   Pixlr-o-matic Support ›

Downloaded ▾   What's New in Version 2.1.2

FX Photo Studio HD

FX Photo Studio ($1.99) is another attempt to find a good balance between ease of use and editing potential. You can use it to apply preset effects to photos. The effects are simple but sophisticated. You can adjust one or two elements in each, and apply effects to selected parts of a photo. You can also apply basic editing including cropping, rotation, and color control. Although FX Photo Studio is not an outstandingly popular app, it is well worth investigating.

App Store › Photo & Video › MacPhun LLC

FX Photo Studio HD
Description

You will be amazed with simplicity and power of FX Photo St
…

MacPhun LLC Web Site ›   FX Photo Studio HD Support ›

Downloaded ▾   What's New in Version 4.0

FX Photo Studio 4.0 is finally here.

CHAPTER 2

Taking and Importing Photos

iPhoto is designed to work with the Camera and Photos apps to take, view, import, and manage photo collections. Use Camera to take photos. Use Photos to view and organize them. You can also import photos from an external camera using the Camera Connection Kit.

Understanding the Camera App

All iPhone and recent iPad devices include at least one built-in camera, and some models include multiple cameras with a built-in LED flash. You can use the Camera app to take photos with these cameras.

Although Camera looks simple, it has some clever hidden features. You can use them to create impressive special effects. Camera is also good for quick snaps and can be accessed through the lock screen without unlocking your device.

Select a Camera

The iPhone 4 and later and the iPad 2 and later include a front camera and a rear camera. You can select either in the Camera app. The front-facing camera is designed for live video with FaceTime, Skype, and similar services. Photo quality is limited, but you can use it to take snaps of yourself without having to use a mirror. The rear-facing camera takes better quality photos. It also works with the LED flash, if your device has one.

Using Camera Controls

iDevice cameras are automatic, so you cannot set the focus, exposure, or shutter speed. However, you can use a manual digital zoom to zoom into part of your photo. You can also tap the photo preview window to force the camera to focus on a small area in the photo. The camera tries to make this area as sharp as possible in the photo, and also uses the brightness of the area to estimate exposure. You can use this feature to create silhouettes, shoot into a bright light, focus on a background and blur a foreground, or deliberately overexpose a photo for special effects.

Using Camera Options

Depending on your iDevice, you can choose various camera options. The *grid* displays a grid that divides the photo preview into nine boxes called *thirds*. This is a standard feature on more expensive cameras. You can use it to improve the composition of your shot. The *HDR* (High Dynamic Range) option is available on the iPhone 4 and later. It combines three photos with different brightness levels into a single photo with enhanced detail in shadows and highlights. The HDR feature is described in Chapter 14.

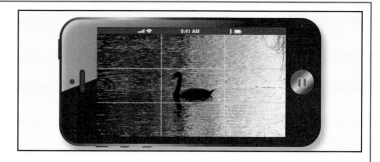

Using the Lock Screen and the Side Button

You need to be quick to catch some photo opportunities. If your iDevice is locked, it can take a while to unlock it, launch the Camera app, and take a snap. To solve this problem, the iPhone includes quick access to Camera on the lock screen, so you can take photos without unlocking your device. Another hidden feature is side button snapping. In some orientations the on-screen button in Camera is awkwardly placed, but the top side button does the same job and is easier to reach. It also has a positive physical click, so you are less likely to move the camera when you use it.

Record Video

Both front and rear cameras — where available — can record video. This option is easy to use. You simply select video or stills with an on-screen switch, and tap the **Recording** button ( ) to begin recording. The button graphics change to remind you what you are capturing. Video quality on the rear camera of the iPhone and 3rd and 4th generation iPads can be surprisingly good.

Take Photos with Camera

You can take a photo with the Camera app by tapping the on-screen snap button or the top side button on the case. The mechanical button is often easier to reach, although you may need to use two hands.

You can also select the forward or rear cameras manually before you take your photo, and on models with a flash, set the flash so it always fires, never fires, or fires only when the light is poor. Not all devices support the extra options. If they are not available, the buttons for them do not appear in the display.

Take Photos with Camera

1 Launch the Camera app by tapping the **Camera** icon on the Home screen.

A iPhoto displays the photo preview window.

2 Move the switch to select the still camera if it is not already selected.

Note: This example uses the iPhone screens because an iPhone is more portable than an iPad. The screen layout is different on the iPad, and some options are not available.

3 Tap the front/rear camera selector icon ( ) to select a camera.

B Camera flips the preview window and shows the view from the other camera.

Note: The front-facing camera is not available on all devices.

Note: Flash and other options are not available when using the front-facing camera.

Note: The front-facing camera usually shows you. (This example deliberately hides the author.)

26

4 Tap the Flash mode button to display the flash options.

Note: The mode button always shows the current flash mode.

5 Tap one of the modes to select it.

Note: Auto mode automatically fires the flash in poor light but does not fire it in good light.

6 Tap the camera icon (📷) to take a photo.

C Camera takes a photo and adds it to the camera roll.

Note: A shutter graphic covers the preview window while Camera takes the photo.

Note: It can take Camera a few seconds to take a photo, especially in poor light. Try to keep the camera still while the shutter is visible.

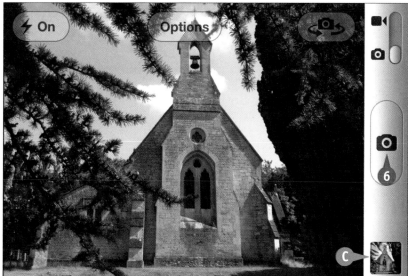

TIPS

Why is there such a difference between the front and rear cameras?
The rear camera is designed for photography. The front camera is really a webcam and is officially called the iSight/FaceTime camera. Use the rear camera when you can. The front camera is good enough for front-facing snaps in good light, but photos from the rear camera always look smoother and more detailed.

Why would I use flash in daylight?
Photographers often use *fill-in flash* in daylight to add extra light to a scene. The built-in flash is not very powerful, but you can still use it for basic fill-in flash. Turn on the flash before you take a photo. If the subject is lit from the side or the rear, the flash adds extra light from the front. The results can be dramatic.

Using Camera Options

You can use a built-in digital zoom to bring distant objects closer before you snap them with the Camera app. You can also display a nine-cell grid to help you frame your photo.

Both options are partly hidden. The zoom feature is slightly awkward to use. You can pinch zoom with two fingers on the photo preview, but you may find it easier to tap with two fingers and drag the zoom slider with a single finger. The other camera options appear when you tap the translucent Options button.

Using Camera Options

1 Launch the Camera app by tapping the **Camera** icon on the Home screen.

A iPhoto displays the photo preview window.

2 Tap the **Options** button to view your camera's options.

B Camera displays options.

3 Tap the **Grid** switch to enable the grid overlay.

4 Tap **Done** to save and hide the options.

Note: You can also tap anywhere on the screen outside the Options box.

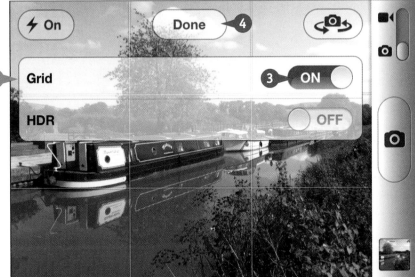

C iPhoto displays a grid of thirds in the photo preview area.

Note: The grid does not appear in your photos.

5 For good results experiment with placing objects and lines in your photos on lines or points on the grid.

Note: The grid is one suggested way to improve your photos, but your photos may still look good with features placed elsewhere.

Note: The HDR option is described in Chapter 14.

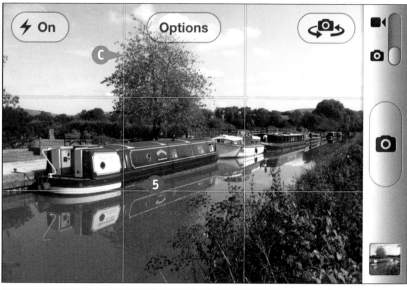

6 Tap with two fingers on the preview window to show the zoom slider.

7 Drag the slider left or right to change the zoom magnification.

Note: You can also pinch and expand with two fingers on the preview, but this often feels less precise than the zoom slider.

Note: As in this example, the photo may look fuzzy if you zoom in too much.

8 Tap the camera icon (📷) to take the photo.

TIPS

Is the zoom digital or optical?
The zoom is digital — it is really a crop. Because camera resolution is limited, the image quality gets worse the more you zoom in. The cameras on the iPhone 4S and 5 are just about good enough to support the maximum zoom. The cameras on earlier iPhones and on iPads can zoom in to around two-thirds of the maximum. If you zoom in further the image becomes very fuzzy.

What is the grid for?
Photographers use the *Rule of Thirds* when composing a shot. Photos often look good when strong lines in the image line up with the lines on the grid, or when important features are on the crossing points. For more details, search the web for "Rule of Thirds."

Control Exposure and Focus

Although you cannot set the camera's exposure and focus manually, you can use a hidden feature to force the camera to look at part of a scene and estimate the brightness and focus from a smaller area.

If you tap once, the camera measures the light in the area you select, but continues to update the exposure if you move the camera or the light changes. If you tap and hold on the screen, the camera locks the exposure and focus. If you move the camera, exposure and focus do not change.

Control Exposure and Focus

1 Launch the Camera app by tapping the **Camera** icon on the Home screen.

A iPhoto displays the photo preview window.

2 Point the camera at brighter or darker parts of a scene. (This example points at a darker area.)

The camera automatically corrects the exposure by measuring the brightness in the entire preview area.

Note: To demonstrate this even more clearly, point the camera at the sun or sky and then the ground.

3 Without moving the camera, tap a darker area in the preview.

Ⓑ Camera displays a small square used to estimate the exposure.

Note: If the area is in shadow, Camera lightens the shot. If the area is brightly lit, Camera darkens the shot. In this mode, Camera ignores the brightness in the rest of the scene.

Note: You can tap again as often as you want to select other areas.

④ Tap and hold with a finger in the preview area.

Ⓒ Camera displays an animated square.

Ⓓ Camera displays the "AE/AF lock" message at the bottom of the preview. AE/AF is short for AutoExposure/AutoFocus.

Note: The exposure and focus are now locked. They no longer follow changes in light or camera position.

⑤ Tap anywhere in the preview area to unlock exposure and focus.

⑥ Tap the camera icon (📷) to take a photo.

TIPS

How can I use this feature?
If you tap and hold a bright area in a scene, you can force the camera to underexpose your photo, creating silhouettes and shadows. If you tap and hold a dark area, you can deliberately create a washed-out look. You can also use this feature to highlight the ground or the sky when snapping landscapes. Tap and hold on the sky, and the camera captures a cloudscape. Tap and hold the landscape and the sky becomes white, but the landscape is exposed correctly.

Is this feature like the AE/AF lock on bigger cameras?
It is the iPhone/iPad equivalent. Unfortunately, you cannot lock focus and exposure separately — they always work together.

Take Photos from the Lock Screen

If you have an iPhone, you can take photos without unlocking it first. You can load the Camera app directly from the lock screen by flicking the camera icon upwards.

Photo opportunities can disappear in moments, but unlocking your iPhone and launching Camera can take a few seconds. You can use the lock screen option to snap a scene quickly before you lose it forever.

Take Photos from the Lock Screen

1 If your phone's display is dark, tap the power button or home button to display the lock screen.

2 Tap and hold the camera icon ().

3 Drag the camera icon (📷) upwards.

Note: Do not drag the unlock slider next to the icon.

Note: The shutter display may appear briefly while Camera launches.

④ Use any of Camera's features to take one or more photos.

Note: All of Camera's features work as normal.

Note: You can rotate your iPhone to take photos in landscape orientation after you unlock it.

⑤ Swipe down in the top half of the preview window to lock your device again.

Note: Swiping in the lower half of the window does nothing.

TIPS

Can I use the top button to take a photo from the lock screen?

Unfortunately not. You must slide the Camera app up from the bottom of the lock screen before you can take a photo with the top button. The button does nothing while the lock screen is visible.

Does this feature work on the iPad?

The iPad does not support the lock screen camera feature. Instead, you can turn your iPad into a digital picture frame. A couple of seconds after you tap the lock screen icon, the iPad displays an animated slide show with photos selected from the albums and events on your device. You can stop the slide show by tapping the screen again and either tapping the slide show icon or unlocking the device.

Record Video

You can record video on all iPhones more recent than the 3G and all iPads from the iPad 2 onwards. Video is saved to the camera roll — described later in this chapter — just like photo stills. To record video, flick a switch in the Camera app. Instead of a camera icon, Camera displays a red button, which flashes as you record.

Video uses more storage space than photos. If you record a lot of video on your device, copy it to a Mac or PC as soon as you can to avoid wasting space.

Record Video

1 Launch the Camera app by tapping the **Camera** icon on the Home screen.

Ⓐ iPhoto displays the photo preview window.

2 Move the switch to select the video camera if it is not already selected.

Ⓑ Camera displays the shutter graphic for a second or so while it changes modes, and also replaces the camera icon with a recording icon with a red LED.

3 Tap the recording icon (●)
to begin recording video.

C Camera beeps once and
flashes the LED while it
records video.

D Camera displays a time
counter so you can see how
much video you have
recorded.

4 Tap the recording icon (●)
again to stop recording
video.

E Camera beeps again and
adds the video to the
camera roll.

5 Tap the camera roll to view
your photos and recordings.

6 Tap the video to prepare it
for playback.

Note: For more information
about previewing and viewing
the camera roll, see the section
later in this chapter.

7 Tap the play icon (▶) to
view the video.

Why do some of the camera options disappear?
Video recording uses a fixed zoom with a small
amount of magnification. You can turn on the
flash to use it as a constant light source for your
video. Other options are not available, so you
cannot use the grid or enable HDR mode.

Can I edit the video?
Camera has no movie editing options. But iMovie
($4.99 from the App Store) includes basic clip
trimming, transitions (that is, clip crossfades and
other animations) and basic support for titles, music
dubbing, and online sharing. If you want to edit
videos, iMovie is an affordable but powerful option.

Understanding Photo Management

iPhoto includes very limited photo management. To manage photos, use the free Photos app. Both apps access the same *photo library*, which holds all the photos on your device.

Photos in the library can be collected into *albums* and *events*. Albums collect photos by theme, and events group photos by import date. Some albums are created automatically. For example, the *camera roll* holds all photos taken with the Camera app. You can create other albums using iPhoto on a Mac, and import them to your device with iTunes. You can also import photos from an attached camera or memory card using the iPad Camera Connection Kit.

Understanding the Photo Library

You can use the photo library to preview every photo on your device. The library appears in Photos and in iPhoto. You can select it by tapping the **Photos** icon on the main page in either app. Both apps display the photos as small thumbnail previews. Photos are sorted in date order using the date the photo was created as a file. Original photos are sorted correctly, but if you copy a photo or save it from a web page, the copy date overrides the original creation date, and the library can easily become a disorganized jumble. Fortunately, photos can be grouped in other ways.

June 06, 2013   June 07, 2013

Understanding Albums and Events

You can get more from the photos in the library by grouping them into collections. You can use albums to collect related photos together — by subject, person, color, mood, or for any other reason. You can tag photos with useful words, and iPhoto automatically groups photos with matching words into albums for you. Your iDevice also creates some albums automatically — for example, iPhoto includes a Beamed album for photos sent manually from other devices. Events organize photos by date. Although you can create albums in Photos, and both iPhoto and Photos can create events, both options are easier to use on a Mac. Many users create albums and events in iPhoto on a Mac or some other application such as Aperture, Photoshop, or Photoshop Elements and use their iDevice as a portable photo album. (For more about creating albums in Photos, see Chapter 5.)

Zoo
June 2013

Gar
Augu

PHOTOS

Understanding the Camera Roll

The camera roll is a special album. The Camera app adds photos to it whenever you take a snap. Some apps, including iPhoto, Mail, and Safari, can also save photos to the camera roll. You can copy the photos on the camera roll to a Mac or PC, upload them to iPhoto on a Mac, or share them to an e-mail, text message, or Twitter post. You can access the camera roll in iPhoto and Photos or indirectly through the Camera app.

Understanding Places

Many cameras including the iPhone and some iPad models embed location information into photos as you take them. The Places feature in the Photos app displays your photo locations on a map with pins for each location. When you zoom out of the map, Places automatically groups nearby locations under a single pin to help keep the display clear and uncluttered. As you zoom in, nearby locations are split and shown with pins of their own. iPhoto on the Mac has an equivalent feature. Unfortunately, iPhoto for iOS does not show places, but if you add photos to a journal, you can show the location of each photo on a separate map. For details see Chapter 13.

Understanding the iPad Camera Connection Kit

The iPad Camera Connection Kit is a pair of adapters that plug into a standard iDevice socket or, via a further optional adapter, into the new iPhone 5 socket. One adapter has a slot for an SD memory card. The other has a standard full-sized flat USB socket. Both adapters work the same way. If you plug in a memory card or a camera via a USB cable, iPhoto imports the photos it finds and collects them into events. The kit is not compatible with the iPhone.

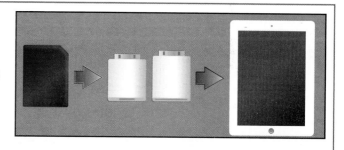

Get Started with the Photos App

Y ou can use the Photos app to view and manage the photos, albums, and events on your device. iPhoto and Photos share the same library so you can see the same photos, albums, and events in both. Use Photos to preview and manage your photos, and iPhoto to edit and enhance them.

Photos is included with every iDevice, so you do not need to download it. It is included on devices that lack a camera, because you can use Photos to view photos, albums and events you download to your device with iTunes.

Get Started with the Photos App

1 Tap the **Photos** icon on the Home screen to launch the Photos app.

2 Tap the **Photos** button to view all the photos in your device library.

3 Tap any photo to view it.

Note: Photos displays a line of mini-thumbnails under a photo when you preview it. The thumbnails fade out after a second or so, and you can view the photo full screen. Tap the screen again to see the thumbnails.

Note: You can view photos by tapping their thumbnails and by swiping left and right.

④ Tap the **Albums** button or the **Events** button to view the albums and events in your device library.

⑤ Tap any album or event to view the photos it holds.

Note: For more about creating and deleting albums in Photos, see Chapter 5.

⑥ Tap the **Places** button to see a map with pins for photo locations.

⑦ Tap a pin to view a popover with a preview of the photo or photos at that location.

⑧ Tap the popover to view all the photos at that location.

Note: If you zoom into a location, more pins may appear. Photos groups nearby locations under a single pin to keep the display uncluttered.

TIPS

Can I edit photos with Photos?

If you tap a photo in Photos and tap the **Edit** button, you can apply Rotate, Enhance, Red-Eye, and Crop tools. These are simpler than the equivalent editing tools in iPhoto, which are described in Chapters 7 to 11 of this book.

When should I use Photos instead of iPhoto?

Photos offers full-screen photo viewing. iPhoto does not. You can select any album or event in Photos, tap to select a photo, and after a couple of seconds the top and bottom tool bars disappear. You can now drag-scroll through that collection, viewing the photos full screen. You can also rotate your device to get the best view in portrait or landscape mode.

Using the Camera Roll

The camera roll is a special album that stores the most recent images added to your iDevice. You can access it through iPhoto, Photos, and — indirectly — through the Camera app. Many third-party photo apps also work with the camera roll.

When you take a photo with your device's camera, the photo is saved to the camera roll. You can also save photos to the camera roll from other sources, including e-mails and web pages.

Using the Camera Roll

1 In Camera, tap the thumbnail in the toolbar to open the camera roll.

Note: You can also open the camera roll by tapping the **Camera Roll** album in iPhoto and Photos.

Note: This example uses the iPad 2 camera.

2 Tap one of the mini-thumbnails to view a photo.

A The camera roll displays the number of the current photo and the total number of photos in the roll.

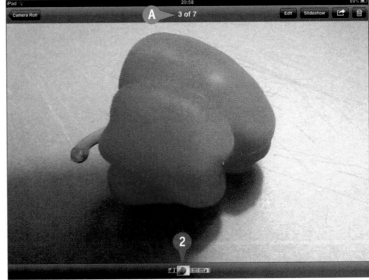

3 Swipe left or right to view other photos in the roll.

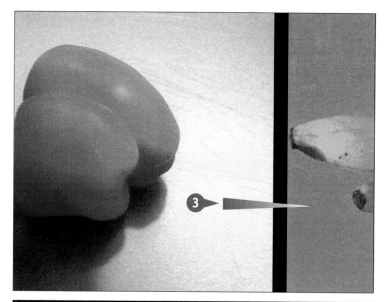

4 Tap the trash can icon (🗑) to delete a photo.

5 Tap **Delete Photo** in the popover to confirm.

Note: There is no Undo option; you cannot recover a photo after you delete it.

Note: You can delete photos only from the camera roll. You cannot delete photos from events or from other albums.

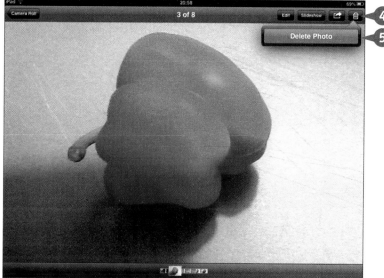

TIPS

How is the camera roll different from other albums?

iDevices have tight security, so you must use special software such as iTunes to copy and manage most of your albums and events. The camera roll works differently. You can copy the photos in it to a Mac or PC. Only the camera roll and the imported photo albums allow this.

Why does iPhoto sometimes display an Updating Photo Library message?

If you add or remove photos from the photo library on your device — for example, by saving photos to the camera roll — iPhoto notices the change and reloads the library automatically to keep it up to date.

Save and Share Photos

Photo includes sophisticated photo sharing options which are introduced in Chapter 12. But you can also save photos from web pages and e-mail to the camera roll, and share any photo in the camera roll to some other destination.

As of iOS 6 you can share photos by e-mail, Twitter, and Facebook. You can also print a photo, save it as your device wallpaper, copy it to paste it into another app, and assign it to an address book contact.

Save and Share Photos

Save a Photo from an E-Mail Message

1 Launch the Mail app from the Home screen.

2 Select any e-mail that includes a photo attachment and tap the photo preview.

3 Tap the **Save Image** icon to save a single image.

A You can tap the **Save Images** icon to save all the images in the e-mail at once.

4 Launch the Photos app and tap the **Camera Roll** album to open it.

5 Tap the most recent mini-thumbnails at the right of the list.

B Photos displays the photo you saved from the e-mail.

Save a Photo from a Website

1 Launch Safari and open a web page.

2 Tap and hold any image on the page.

Note: Images can be any size, anywhere on the page. They do not have to fill the screen.

3 Tap **Save Image** to save the image to the camera roll.

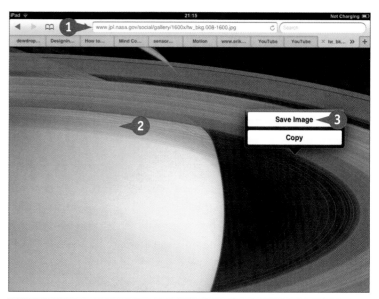

Share a Photo

1 Return to Photos and view the camera roll album.

2 Tap the **Share** icon ( ) to share a photo.

3 Tap one of the options in the popover to select a sharing option.

iPhoto displays a sharing tool for each option. For more details, see Chapter 12.

TIPS

Are uploaded photos full sized?

Between them, iPhoto and Facebook shrink photos to a manageable size, usually a few hundred pixels on a side. iPhoto does not upload the original full-sized versions of your photos. Although web users can still download and link to your photos, they cannot make high-resolution prints or copies.

Do the photos include location information?

iPhoto uploads location information to Facebook, and you can add a location to the photo on Facebook if you choose to. However, location information is stripped out of the photo. If someone downloads a photo, he cannot see your location.

Using the Camera Connection Kit

You can use Apple's optional Camera Connection Kit to import photos into your device. The official Apple version of the kit includes two connectors — one with a slot for an SD card and one with a standard USB socket. The Camera Connection Kit can read JPEG, PNG, and RAW format files.

To get started, plug one end of the connector into your device's main port. Insert an SD card or connect a USB camera — you can use another iDevice as a source. The Photos app launches automatically. You can then start importing your photos.

Using the Camera Connection Kit

1 Plug one of the connectors into the main port of your device.

Note: This example uses a single combined budget non-Apple connector with a built-in card reader and USB socket.

2 Insert a card into the slot.

3 If you are using a combined reader with a switch, set the switch to the SD or Card position.

4 Alternatively, plug a connector with a USB socket into your device.

5 Connect your camera with a USB cable that matches its socket.

Note: Many cameras use the "Mini-B" plug shown here. Some use smaller plugs called "Micro-AB" or "Micro-B." Check your camera's manual for details.

6 Plug the end of the USB cable with the standard plug into the connector.

7 Set the side switch to USB, if necessary.

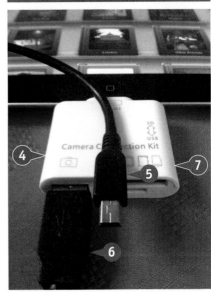

The Photos app launches automatically.

Photos begins to load preview images from the camera or card, and displays a grid of empty thumbnails and a Loading icon.

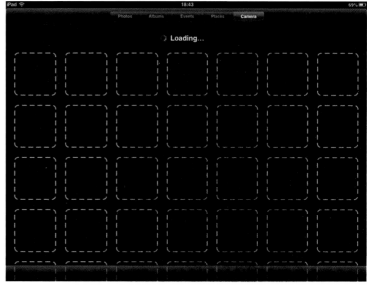

After a while, typically a few minutes, Photos finishes loading the thumbnails.

8 Tap **Import All** to begin importing the photos.

A You can alternatively tap **Delete All** to clear the photos from the card or camera.

Note: If you delete the photos, you lose them forever.

TIPS

Which memory cards and cameras are supported?

The official Apple Camera Connection Kit supports SD and SDHC cards. SDXC cards do not work. You can use CF and other flash cards with a separate non-Apple converter — look on Amazon, eBay, and photo accessory stores. Most cameras with a USB connector are compatible with the USB adapter. You can also import photos from any USB drive or supported card by copying them to a folder named DCIM.

Can I buy a cheaper adapter?

eBay and Amazon sell budget alternatives of the official Apple Camera Connection Kit. Many are all-in-one designs that combine a USB socket with a card reader. Some have extra slots for a wider range of memory cards. Prices are extremely low compared to the Apple model, but reliability cannot be guaranteed.

continued ▶   **45**

When you use the Camera Connection Kit, the Photos app launches automatically and displays a grid of thumbnails. You cannot pick and choose the photos you want — you must import them all, or cancel the import completely. As the photos import, Photos marks them with a green check mark. After import you can choose to keep the photos on the source or delete them. Photos automatically creates Last Import and All Imported albums, and splits the photos into events by date. You can view the albums and events in Photos or in iPhoto.

Using the Camera Connection Kit (continued)

Photos begins to import the photos. Each photo is marked with a green check after import.

Ⓐ You can optionally tap **Stop Import** to end the import.

Note: Photos keeps the photos already imported if you stop early.

Ⓑ Photos asks if you want to delete the photos from your card or camera.

⑨ Tap **Keep** to keep the photos.

Ⓒ You can tap **Delete** to delete the photos.

Note: You cannot recover the photos if you delete them.

10 Tap the **Events** button.

D Photos automatically splits the photos into events grouped by date.

Note: All the photos taken on the same date appear in a single event.

11 Tap the **Albums** button.

12 Tap the **Last Import** album to open it.

Photos automatically collects all the photos from the last import into this album.

Note: Photos also creates an album called All Imported, which holds photos from every import.

Note: Import does not rotate photos, so if any of your photos are sideways you must rotate them manually in iPhoto or Photos.

TIPS

Can I add imported photos to an album?
You cannot add the imported photos to an existing album. However, you can create a completely new album and add as many photos as you want to that. You also cannot add the new photos to an existing event.

What happens when I next sync my device?
iTunes does not automatically import the new photos, events, or albums to your Mac. Photos in the Last Import and All Imported albums can be imported to a Mac or PC just like the photos on your camera roll, but they are not grouped into albums. If you have iPhoto for the Mac, you can place them into albums by hand.

Copy Photos to a Mac or PC

You can copy the photos in your camera roll and all photos imported with the Camera Connection Kit from your device to a Mac or PC. To access photos in albums or events, use the sharing options introduced in Chapter 12.

Use manual copying if you do not have iPhoto for the Mac or if you are using a PC. A device plugged into a PC appears as an external USB drive. This option is not available on a Mac, but you can import the photos using an application called Image Capture.

Copy Photos to a Mac or PC

Copy Photos to a Mac

1 Plug your device into your Mac.

2 Open the **Applications** folder in Finder.

3 Double-click the **Image Capture** application.

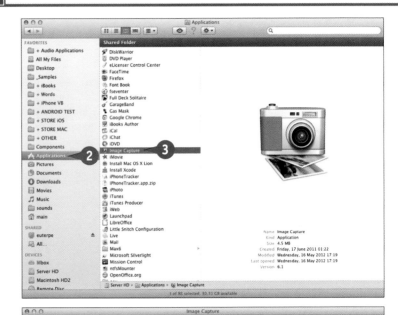

4 Use the file selector to choose a folder for your photos.

5 Click **Import All** to import all photos.

A You can press and hold **Shift** on the keyboard and click single photos to select them and then click **Import** to import the selected photos.

Note: You can use the connection and delete options at the bottom left to choose what happens on connection and import.

Copy Photos to a PC

1 On a PC, plug your device into a USB socket.

The AutoPlay dialog box appears.

2 Click **Open device to view files**.

Note: You may need to scroll down a list to see this option.

B You can optionally click **Always do this for this device** (☐ changes to ☑) to view the files automatically without seeing the dialog box.

Note: If you have image editing software installed, you may be able to import the photos into it directly.

3 Click through the folders on the device until you open the folder at the lowest level inside the DCIM (Digital Camera Import) folder.

4 Drag some or all of the photos from the device and drop them into any other folder.

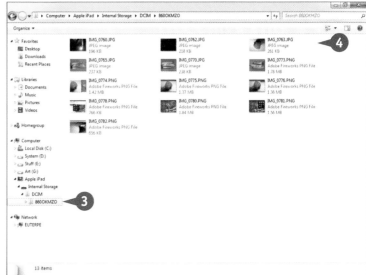

TIPS

Can I copy photos from a computer to the device?

You cannot add photos to a device. To import photos on a Mac or PC for viewing, use iTunes. On a Mac, you can import photos from the Pictures folder or from the Mac version of iPhoto. On a PC you can select a folder by name. Copying photos adds them to an event or folder, but not to the camera roll.

Why is there no way to file-copy photos on a Mac?

For security reasons, Apple devices are locked to specific software. When you plug your device into your Mac, it does not appear in Finder as a USB drive. You can access the photos on the camera roll only through iTunes and Image Capture.

CHAPTER 3

Using iCloud and Photo Stream

You can use Photo Stream to share photos automatically between devices that have Wi-Fi. You do not need to remember to beam photos or share them by hand. You must remember to save the photos on a device before they disappear.

Understanding Photo Stream

Photo Stream is Apple's simplest and most straightforward photo sharing tool. Photo Stream is like a shared album. It uses iCloud technology to share photos automatically between devices. When you take or upload a photo, iCloud copies it to other devices with the same iCloud account.

Photo Stream works almost effortlessly, but it can be easy to miss that it is a synchronization tool, not a giant Internet hard drive. Photo Stream copies photos between devices. Although you can create small online galleries with Photo Stream, it is not an alternative to online photo sharing sites such as Flickr or Picasa.

Understanding iCloud

Photo Stream relies on iCloud technology to manage photo copying. To use iCloud, you must have an Apple ID, which is usually the same as your iTunes and App Store ID. You must enable iCloud and log in with your ID on every device you want to use for photo sharing, including handheld devices, Macs, and PCs. Once Photo Stream is working, photos pass through iCloud to every device. iCloud does not keep the photos it shares. Instead, it checks if all connected devices have the same images, and copies photos between them until they do. Note that although other iCloud traffic may use your cellular connection, photo sharing always works over Wi-Fi. Photo Stream does not affect your iCloud storage allowance.

Understanding Photo Sharing

When you share a photo with Photo Stream, it automatically appears on other devices with a Wi-Fi connection and the same iCloud account. (In iOS 6, you can share photos between multiple accounts.) You can share photos in various ways. If you take a photo with the Camera app or save a photo from some other source to the camera roll, Photo Stream shares it automatically. You can also share photos from a Mac or PC. You can even use Photo Stream to share photos between Macs, PCs, and an Apple TV.

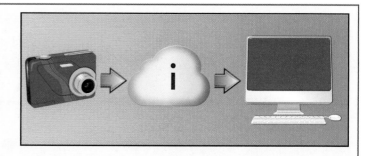

Understanding Photo Stream on a Device

On a device, both incoming and outgoing shared photos appear in a special My Photo Stream album in iPhoto. Streamed photos also appear in the Photos app in a special Photo Stream collection. Because device memory is limited, the Photo Stream album keeps only the last 1,000 shared photos. It also deletes 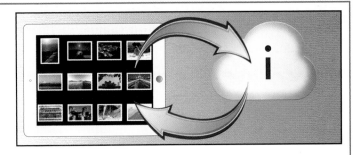 photos that were streamed more than 30 days ago. If you want to keep streamed photos for longer, you must move them to another album using iPhoto on a Mac or equivalent Mac or PC software and then reimport them with iTunes.

Understanding Photo Stream on a Mac

On a Mac, Photo Stream offers unlimited storage. Photos are never deleted automatically, and you can keep as many you take. Once you set up Photo Stream on a Mac, you can open the Photo Stream album to view photos streamed from devices. You can also copy photos to your devices by dragging them from your Mac's iPhoto collection into the  Photo Stream album. This option is a great way to share a small number of photos with a device without having to synchronize them through iTunes. However, you cannot stream albums or events — iTunes sync is the only way to copy these items to a device.

Understanding Photo Stream on a PC

If you install iCloud on a PC and turn on Photo Stream, photos are copied to a special Photo Stream folder in the Pictures folder on your PC. Photo Stream on a PC is less sophisticated than the Mac version. You cannot share photos from a PC application, but you can copy photos from a digital camera over USB into the Photo Stream 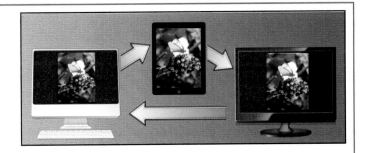 upload folder to share them with your devices or with a Mac.

Set up Photo Stream for iOS

You can set up Photo Stream for iOS in the Settings app. When Photo Stream is running, iPhoto, Photos, and the Camera app send and receive photos automatically. You do not need to select them or send them manually.

You must enable Wi-Fi before you use Photo Stream. If Wi-Fi is not available immediately, Photo Stream queues new photos and syncs them when your device discovers a Wi-Fi connection. If you never enable Wi-Fi, Photo Stream cannot work.

Set up Photo Stream for iOS

1 Launch the Settings app on your device.

2 Tap the **Wi-Fi** option.

Settings displays the Wi-Fi options.

3 If Wi-Fi is not already running, tap the switch to enable it.

4 If a network is available, tap it to connect to it.

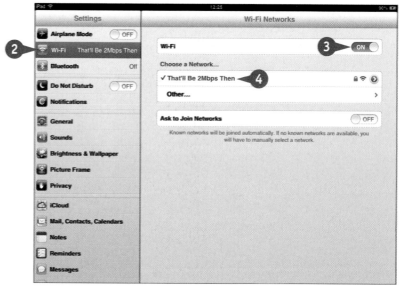

5 Tap the **iCloud** option.

iPhoto displays the iCloud settings.

6 Tap the **Photo Stream** option.

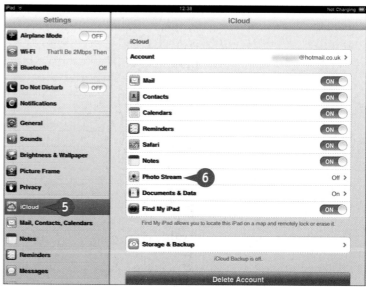

Settings displays the Photo Stream options.

7 Tap the switch to enable your personal Photo Stream.

8 Optionally, tap the **Shared Photo Streams** switch to enable shared photo streams.

Note: You can create a shared photo stream without enabling your personal photo stream, although this is not usually a useful option.

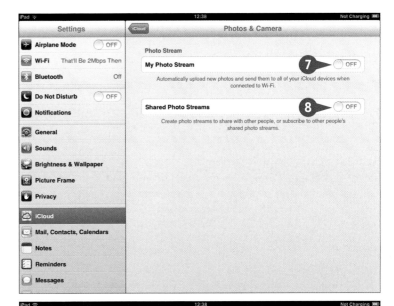

A iPhoto enables either or both options and Photo Stream starts working.

Note: You do not need to change any settings in iPhoto, Photos, or the Camera app.

TIPS

Does saving a photo from a web page send it to Photo Stream?
Yes. If you tap and hold on any image in Safari in iOS and then tap the **Save Image** option, the photo is saved to your camera roll and sent out over Photo Stream. Photo Stream also works with any photo from any other source such as a document. Every photo added to the camera roll is synced.

How quick is Photo Stream?
Photo Stream is fast, but not instant. A single new photo usually appears in a minute or so. If your Wi-Fi connection is slow or if you upload a lot of photos quickly, it can take much longer for Photo Stream to catch up. For best performance avoid uploading tens of photos at once. Syncing many photos can take a very long time.

Set up Photo Stream on a Mac

You can set up iPhoto on a Mac to work with Photo Stream. Once iPhoto is running, photos from devices appear automatically in the Photo Stream collection in iPhoto for Mac. You can also drag any photo onto the Photo Stream item to share it with your devices, or even with another Mac.

To set up Photo Stream, open the iCloud item in the System Preferences and enable the Photo Stream option. Once you enable Photo Stream, sharing begins automatically.

Set up Photo Stream on a Mac

1 Click ![Apple menu] and then **System Preferences** to open the System Preferences application.

2 Double-click **iCloud** to open it.

System Preferences shows the iCloud settings.

3 If you are not already logged in, enter your iCloud account e-mail address or Apple ID and password.

4 Click **Sign In**.

Note: The Sign In button stays grayed out until you enter an Apple ID and password.

iCloud signs you in.

5 Click the **Photo Stream** check box in the list of iCloud options (☐ changes to ☑).

iCloud enables Photo Stream.

Note: Unless you also have iPhoto open, iCloud does not give you any other warning that Photo Stream is running.

6 Launch iPhoto.

7 Click the **Photo Stream** item.

Ⓐ Streamed photos from devices appear automatically in this area.

Note: You can also drag any photo and drop it on the Photo Stream item to copy it to your stream and all the devices connected to it.

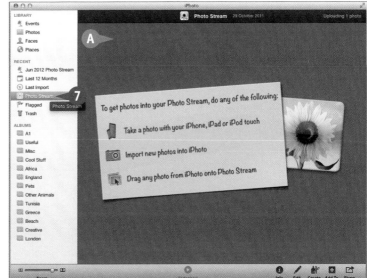

TIPS

Does Photo Stream work only with iPhoto?
You might expect Photo Stream to sync your Mac's Pictures folder, but it does not. However, it does work with Apple's professional Aperture photo application. You can share photos from Aperture in much the same way as you can share them with iPhoto.

Does Photo Stream work on all Macs?
iCloud is built into OS X Lion 10.7.2 and later. The latest features, including sharing to multiple iCloud accounts, are available only with OS X Mountain Lion.

Set up Photo Stream in Windows

You can install Photo Stream on a recent Windows PC and use it to send and receive photos from your Photo Stream. Photo Stream is not currently supported by any Windows photo or design applications, but you can still use it to copy photos to and from your devices. You can also use it to share photos with a Mac, or with another PC.

Because there is no application support, Photo Stream copies photos to and from a pair of folders on your PC. You can select the folders you want to share. Copying photos from a digital camera into the Upload folder shares them automatically.

Set up Photo Stream in Windows

1 Open your favorite browser and search the web for the current download location of the iCloud Control Panel for Windows.

Note: At this writing, the URL is http://support.apple.com/kb/DL1455.

2 Right click the installer and save it to your PC.

3 Double-click the installer to launch it.

4 Click **Next** and follow the steps to complete the installation.

The installer installs the iCloud Control Panel on your PC.

5 Enter your Apple ID and password.

6 Click **Sign in**.

Note: The Sign In button stays grayed out until you enter an Apple ID and password.

7 Click the **Photo Stream** check box to enable Photo Stream (☐ changes to ☑).

8 Click the **Options** button to select Photo Stream's upload and download folders.

9 Click **Change** to select a different folder for the upload and/or download folders, and navigate to the new folder in Windows Explorer.

10 Click **OK** when done.

11 Click **Apply** in the previous dialog box to set the folders and launch Photo Stream.

The iCloud Control Panel launches Photo Stream. Photos from devices appear in the download folder. Photos you copy to the upload folder appear on connected devices.

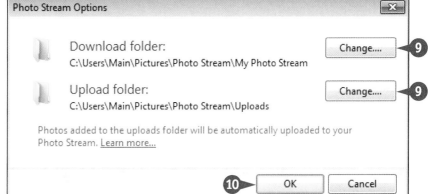

TIPS

Can I use any version of Windows?
Photo Stream works with iCloud, so your PC must be running Windows Vista SP2, Windows 7, or Windows 8. Windows XP and earlier versions are not supported.

Can I use iCloud's other features on Windows?
You can use iCloud on the PC to share contacts, your calendar, email, and other information with Macs and with your handheld devices. If you use both Macs and PCs, iCloud makes data sharing simple and convenient.

Add Photos to Photo Stream

Once Photo Stream is running, you can add photos to it by taking a photo on a device, uploading photos into iPhoto, dragging photos from your Mac's iPhoto collection to the Photo Stream item, or by saving photos from other sources to the camera roll on a device.

Whenever you add photos, they are shared automatically with all connected devices. Because Photo Stream works over Wi-Fi, devices do not have to be close to each other. You can take photos anywhere and your photos will often get home before you do.

Add Photos to Photo Stream

Take Photos on a Device and Add Them to Photo Stream

1. On a device, launch the Camera app.

2. Tap the camera icon (📷) to take a photo.

   If Wi-Fi is available, Photo Stream shares the photo immediately. If not, Photo Stream waits until your device has a Wi-Fi connection.

Share Photos from a Device Using iPhoto on a Mac

1. In iPhoto on a Mac, connect a device with photos on its camera roll and wait until it is recognized.

2. Click the **Import Photos** button to import the photos.

   Photo Stream shares the photos as soon as they are imported.

Note: If Photo Stream is already running on the device you are importing from, iPhoto reports that the photos have already been uploaded, so you do not need to upload them again.

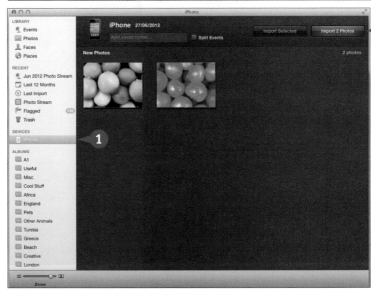

Share Other Photos from Your Mac's iPhoto Library to Photo Stream

1 In iPhoto on a Mac, select a photo or a range of photos.

2 Drag and drop the photo(s) on the Photo Stream item in the list at the left.

Photo Stream shares the photos.

View the Shared Photos

1 To view the shared photos in iPhoto on a device, open the Albums list.

2 Tap the **My Photo Stream** album to open it.

A The streamed photos appear in the My Photo Stream album. You can tap any thumbnail to view a photo.

Note: In iPhoto on a Mac, click the **Photo Stream** item in the list at the left of the page to view the stream.

TIPS

Can I choose which photos are added to Photo Stream?
In iOS 5, all camera roll photos are streamed. You cannot select certain photos only. In iOS 6, the sharing option in the Photos app includes a new selective streaming feature. You can select certain photos for streaming and e-mail the recipients a link to the stream. To use selective streaming, select any photo or group of photos in the Photos view, tap the share option at the top left of the toolbar (top right for a single photo), tap **Photo Stream**, and either create a new stream or add the photos to an existing stream.

Does Photo Stream slow down my Mac?
Photo Stream uses a lot of processor power. On slower Macs you may notice that other applications run more slowly when Photo Stream is enabled and iPhoto is running.

Delete Photos from Photo Stream

You can delete photos from a Photo Stream using the Photos app on a device. iPhoto does not include a delete option.

When you delete a photo from Photo Stream, it disappears from the Photo Stream album on all devices. Deleting a photo from a camera roll does not remove it from Photo Stream. Similarly, deleting a new photo from Photo Stream does not remove it from the camera roll. When Photo Stream is running you must delete a photo from the camera roll and from Photo Stream to get rid of it completely.

Delete Photos from Photo Stream

1 Launch the Photos app.

2 Tap the **Photo Stream** button to open it.

Photos displays a list of streams, including My Photo Stream.

3 Tap **My Photo Stream** to open it.

Note: My Photo Stream is the main shared stream for your iCloud account. If you have created shared streams for friends and relatives they also appear on this page.

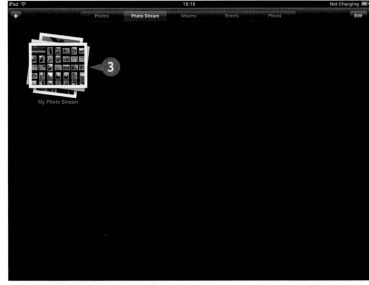

Photos displays thumbnails of the photos in the stream.

④ Tap the **Edit** button.

⑤ Tap photos to select them for deletion.

Photos marks the selected photos with a check.

⑥ Tap **Delete** to remove the photos from the stream.

⑦ Tap **Delete Selected Photos** to confirm the deletion.

Photo Stream deletes the photos from the stream on all connected devices.

Note: Photo Stream deletions are permanent. There is no Undo option.

Do edited photos count as a separate photo?
Edited and original photos are separate. If you delete an original photo from a stream, edited versions stay in the stream and vice versa.

Does deleting a photo from a stream delete it from albums and photo collections?
Photo Stream is a portable shared album. You can add and remove photos from it just as you can with any other album. The photos remain on your device and in other collections even if you delete them from a stream.

Reset Photo Stream

You may sometimes want to remove all Photo Stream photos from your devices and start from scratch.

Deleting all photos is a two-stage process. First, log in to the iCloud website and reset Photo Stream for your account. This step deletes photos that have not synced across all devices. Next, turn Photo Stream off and on again on every device. This deletes the photos in the Photo Stream album. After both steps, Photo Stream is empty and you can start adding photos again.

Reset Photo Stream

1 Open a web browser with the following URL: www.icloud.com.

2 If you have not signed in to iCloud before, click the **Sign In** button.

3 Type your iCloud username.

4 Type your iCloud password.

5 Click the arrow ( ).

Note: You can optionally click **Keep me signed in** to stay signed in (☐ changes to ☑).

iCloud signs you in. You can now use other iCloud online services.

6 Click your account name.

iCloud displays a dialog with various options.

7 Click the **Advanced** option.

8 Click **Reset Photo Stream**.

9 Click **Reset** to confirm.

Note: You may also be asked to enter your password again.

iCloud resets the Photo Stream and ends any pending copy operations.

10 To delete all Photo Stream photos from a device, turn off Photo Stream on the device, and then turn it on again.

The Photo Stream album is emptied on every device.

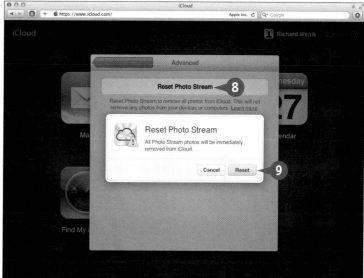

TIPS

Why is there no Photo Stream icon on icloud.com?

icloud.com does not include your photo stream, and you cannot view photos online. This is because Photo Stream is not an online file space. It is a sharing tool. Photos in your streams are stored on your devices, not on Apple's servers.

Why do I need to turn Photo Stream off and on again?

It would be convenient if iCloud could send a reset command to every device, but this feature is not available in the current version. When you turn off Photo Stream on a device, the Photo Stream album is cleared automatically. Unfortunately, the only way to remove streamed photos from a device is to turn off Photo Stream to delete the photos, and then turn it back on again.

CHAPTER 4

Introducing Photo Browsing

You can use iPhoto's browser to preview photos, collect photos for sharing, and select photos for editing. The browser displays a grid of *thumbnails* — small preview photos. You can change the thumbnail display to suit the way you work.

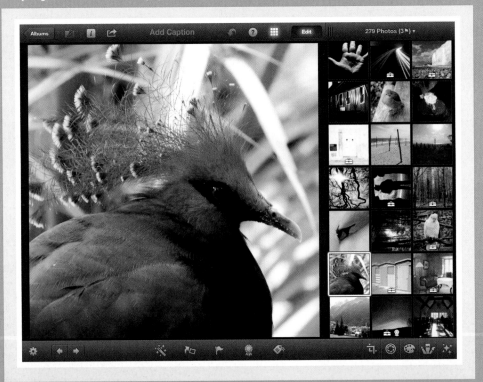

Understanding Photo Browsing

You can use Photo Browsing to preview your photos and select them for editing. All of iPhoto's main features, including simple and advanced editing, tagging, flagging, and sharing, are built into the browser.

To use the browser, first select an album, event, or photo collection on the main page. Tap to open it. The browser displays the photos for that item only. To browse all the photos on your device, select the Photos item.

Understanding Thumbnails

The browser displays *thumbnails* — small photo previews arranged on a grid. You can change the size and position of the grid and hide it completely to leave more — or less — room for photo previews. When you edit or tag a photo (see Chapter 6 for details) iPhoto adds a small white symbol to the photo's thumbnail. You can use this feature to see at a glance which photos are modified, which are favorites, and so on.

Understanding Previews

To view a photo, tap its thumbnail. iPhoto loads a larger version of the photo into the main preview area on the screen. You can now edit the photo, share it, or view information about it. Note that although the Photos app has a full-screen preview option, iPhoto does not. You can hide the edit buttons along the bottom of the screen, but you cannot hide the top toolbar.

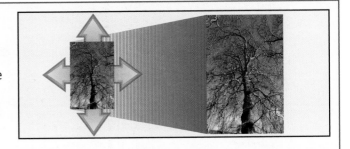

Understanding Photo Selection

You can select more than one photo at a time. You cannot edit more than one photo at once, but you can tag multiple photos, share them, or add them to a journal. You can also search for visually similar photos. Some of the selection options are invisible — you can find out about them later in this chapter.

Introducing the Thumbnail Browser

You can use the options in the thumbnail browser to rearrange the thumbnail view. You can also access the main editing tools, caption your photo, and use the tagging features described in Chapter 6.

Ⓐ Thumbnails Grid

Displays a scrollable list of small photo previews.

Ⓑ Selected Thumbnail

A selected thumbnail is outlined with a white box.

Ⓒ Show/Hide Icon

Tap this icon to show or hide the thumbnails grid.

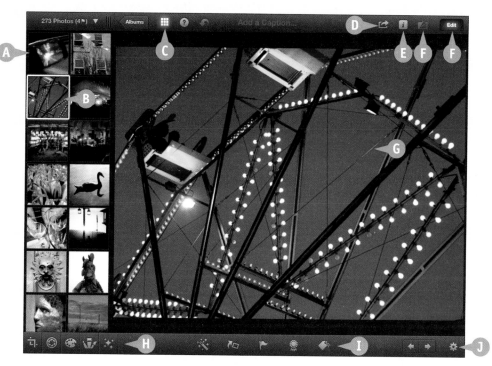

Ⓓ Share Icon

Tap this icon to display iPhoto's sharing options.

Ⓔ Info Icon

Tap this icon to display info about the photo.

Ⓕ Edit Options

Tap to select edit mode and show or hide edits.

Ⓖ Preview Area

Selected photos appear here.

Ⓗ Edit Icons

Tap to use iPhoto's advanced editing features.

Ⓘ Main Toolbar

Tap these icons for simple edits and for tagging and flagging.

Ⓙ Supporting Tools

Scroll through the photos and select further options.

View Single Photos

You can select a single photo by tapping its thumbnail, by swiping through the thumbnails, or by tapping a pair of buttons to step through the thumbnails.

When you select a photo, iPhoto automatically resizes it to fill the preview area. You can now edit the photo, share it, or check its information to find out about the camera and settings used to take the photo. Or you can simply look at it. Note that there is no full-screen preview option, but you can hide the bottom toolbar by tapping the **Edit** button at the top right.

View Single Photos

1 Select an album or event or the Photos collection on the main page.

iPhoto displays the photos in the item you selected.

2 If the thumbnail grid is not visible, tap the **Show/Hide Thumbnails** icon (▦).

3 Tap any thumbnail to display a photo in the main preview area.

iPhoto displays the photo.

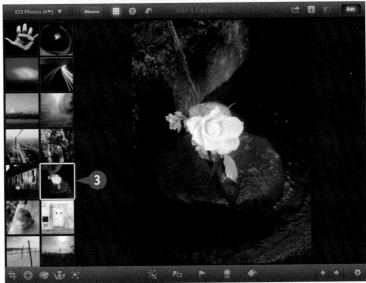

4 Swipe left or right to view the previous or next photo in the list.

5 Tap one of the previous or next buttons to view the previous or next photo in the thumbnails list.

iPhoto displays the previous or next photo.

TIPS

Can I zoom into part of a photo?
You can use a two-finger pinch in the preview area to zoom into and out of a photo to view details. You can also use a two-finger rotation to rotate a photo. The two gestures are similar, so practice pinching to avoid rotating your photos by accident. You can double-tap part of a photo to zoom in and double-tap again to zoom out.

Is there a difference between swipe scrolling and button scrolling?
Many users feel that swipe-scrolling feels quicker and more natural than button scrolling because the scroll buttons are small. If you swipe to scroll, you can cancel the swipe before the next photo appears by lifting your finger. iPhoto "un-scrolls" the preview window to show the original photo.

Introducing the Thumbnail Grid

You can set up the thumbnail grid to maximize space for previews, or hide it altogether. The default width shows two thumbnails, but you can set the width to display between one and four thumbnails instead. You can also move the thumbnail grid to the left or the right of the preview area.

The thumbnail toolbar includes extra photo filtering features that work with iPhoto's tagging and flagging features. You can use these to show a selection of thumbnails. For details, see Chapter 6.

Introducing the Thumbnail Grid

① Open the thumbnail browser.

Note: See the previous section to open the thumbnail browser.

② Tap and hold the divider at the top of the thumbnail grid.

③ Slide it to the left and release it.

iPhoto displays a single column of thumbnails.

④ Tap and hold the divider again.

⑤ Slide it to the right and release it.

iPhoto displays two, three, or four columns of thumbnails.

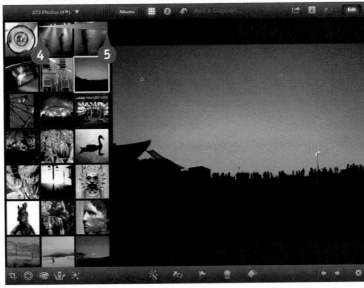

6 Tap and hold the thumbnail toolbar.

7 Drag it to the right of the screen and release it.

iPhoto moves the thumbnail grid to the right edge of the screen.

Note: Be careful to tap the toolbar, not the divider or the disclosure triangle.

8 Tap the **Show/Hide Thumbnails** icon (▦) for the thumbnail grid.

Ⓐ iPhoto hides the thumbnails and resizes the photo so it almost fills the screen.

Note: You can tap the **Show/Hide Thumbnails** icon again to show the thumbnails.

Note: You can also show and hide the thumbnail grid by tapping and dragging the edge next to the preview area.

Why can I move the thumbnails to either side of the screen?
Some users are left-handed, whereas others find it more comfortable to keep the thumbnails on the right-hand side of the screen. If you prefer the thumbnails at the left, you can ignore this feature.

Can I move the thumbnails to the top or bottom of the screen?
In landscape mode, the thumbnails can be placed only on either side of the preview area. If you rotate your device to portrait mode, the thumbnails automatically move to the bottom of the screen. You cannot move them to the top. In portrait mode, you can view up to five thumbnail rows by dragging the horizontal divider. You can also scroll through them vertically, which is a very quick way to preview the thumbnails list.

Select Multiple Photos by Dragging

You can preview multiple photos in the preview area. This is a good way to select photos before you share them or add them to a journal. You can also use this feature to tag and flag multiple photos.

You can drag photos to the preview area to select more than one photo a time. To deselect a photo from a multiple preview, swipe down on it. You can also double-select a photo in a group preview to view it at maximum size. Double selection adds a double-width border around a thumbnail.

Select Multiple Photos by Dragging

1 Open the thumbnail browser.

2 Tap a photo to select it.

iPhoto displays the photo in the preview area.

3 Drag another thumbnail from the grid onto the preview area.

iPhoto displays both photos, resizes them automatically to make them fit, and draws a thin white selection frame around both thumbnails.

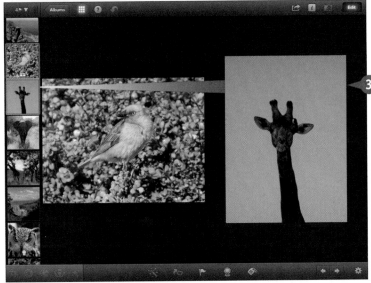

④ Repeat step **3** and drag further thumbnails into the preview area.

iPhoto displays the other photos, resizing them as needed.

Note: You can add any thumbnail from any position in the list, in any order.

⑤ Tap a thumbnail to double-select a photo and expand it to fill the preview area.

Note: You can also tap any photo in the preview area to expand it.

⑥ Tap the photo or its thumbnail again to restore multiple previews.

⑦ Tap any unselected thumbnail to remove the multiple selections.

Note: You can swipe down on a photo to remove it from a multiple selection without deselecting the others.

TIPS

How many photos can I preview at once?
You can view up to 12 photos in the preview area. If you select more than 12 photos, iPhoto previews the first 11 and adds a message at the bottom right-hand corner telling you that further photos are selected but not shown. You cannot view these photos — there is no way to scroll the previews.

Can I zoom and rotate the photos?
If you pinch-zoom any photo in a multiple preview, you can zoom into it. You can also drag the zoomed area inside its frame. The size of the frame does not change. You can also use a two-finger rotation gesture to rotate a photo.

Select Multiple Photos by Tapping

You can select photos for multiple preview by tapping and holding their thumbnails.

Although to some users dragging feels slightly more natural than tapping, the latter offers extra features, more positive responses, and more control. For example, you can remove a single photo from the preview list by tapping it and holding it.

Select Multiple Photos by Tapping

1 Open the thumbnail browser.

2 Tap a thumbnail to preview a photo.

iPhoto displays the photo in the preview area.

3 Tap and hold another thumbnail.

A iPhoto adds the second photo to the preview area.

4 Repeat step **3** to add further photos.

iPhoto adds the photos to the preview area.

Note: You can add any thumbnail from any position in the list, in any order.

5 Tap and hold a selected thumbnail to remove it from the preview list.

iPhoto deselects the photo and removes it from the preview area.

Note: Be careful to tap and hold the photo. If you tap without holding, iPhoto either double-selects a photo if it is already selected, or cancels the multiple selection.

TIPS

Can I select a range of photos?
You can, but not by tapping with two fingers. iPhoto includes a range selection option, but it is slightly hidden. For details, see the next section.

Can I combine tapping with dragging?
You can use either gesture to add a photo to the preview area. iPhoto does not remember which gesture you used, so you always can tap and hold a photo to deselect it from a multiple preview, even if you added it by dragging.

Select a Range of Photos

You can use a partially hidden feature in iPhoto to select a range of photos. Selecting a range saves you time. You can select the first and last photos in the range, and iPhoto automatically selects the photos between them.

You can also use this feature to select individual photos by tapping them once to select them and tapping them again to deselect them. When you tap **Done**, iPhoto adds all selected photos to the preview area.

Select a Range of Photos

1. Open the thumbnail browser.

2. Tap the settings (gear) icon (⚙).

3. Tap the **Select Multiple** option.

Note: If the settings (gear) icon is not visible, tap the **Edit** button near the top right of the screen.

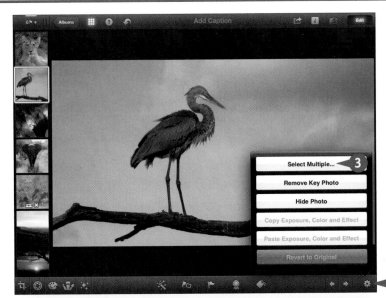

iPhoto opens the Range page.

4. Tap the **Range** button.

5. Tap the first photo in the range you want to select.

   iPhoto highlights the photo with a white border and marks it with a check mark.

Note: You cannot use any of the editing tools or tagging and flagging features while the Range page is open.

6 Tap the last photo in the range you want to select.

A iPhoto highlights all photos in the range with a check mark.

Note: You can scroll up and down the thumbnails and select any photo as the end of the range.

7 Tap **Done**.

B iPhoto hides the range selection page and adds all the photos in the range to the preview area.

Do I have to select a range?

When you use the Select Multiple feature, you can select individual photos by tapping them. This feature is similar to the tap and hold selection option in the previous section, with three differences: selected photos are not added to the preview area until you tap **Done**; selected photos are highlighted with a check mark; and you can tap photos to select them without having to hold them. Although using Select Multiple adds an extra couple of taps, it is the most flexible and powerful way to select multiple photos.

Using the Loupe

iPhoto includes a virtual magnifying glass called a *loupe*. The loupe looks and works like a small magnifying lens. You can drag it over a photo to magnify a small area.

Professional photographers use a glass loupe to highlight details and look for flaws on paper prints. You can use the virtual loupe in the same way. The loupe's small size is fixed and you can only use it to magnify a preview. You cannot use it to work on a small part of a photo while editing.

Using the Loupe

1 Tap any photo to select it and view it in the preview area.

2 Close two fingers, and then tap and hold them on the preview area at the same time.

Note: You may find it takes practice to get the gesture to work for you. Try to move your fingers as little as possible after tapping.

iPhoto displays the loupe and magnifies the area you selected.

3 Drag the loupe over the photo to move it and magnify a different area.

Note: You can drag the rim of the loupe or the magnified "lens" area.

4 Place two fingers inside the loupe area and rotate them to change the magnification.

Note: Rotate clockwise to increase magnification and counterclockwise to decrease it.

Note: When the loupe first appears, rotating counterclockwise does nothing because the magnification is already as low as it can be.

5 When done, tap anywhere on the photo or on the loupe to make it disappear.

iPhoto hides the loupe.

TIPS

Can I use the loupe on multiple photos?
The loupe works only on a single preview. You cannot use it when multiple photos are selected. However, you can pinch-zoom into any selected photo in the preview area. The size of the photo's frame is fixed, but you can zoom in to magnify an area and drag the magnified view within the frame.

Can I use the loupe on a zoomed photo?
You can usually use the loupe on a photo you have already pinch-zoomed. However, the loupe does not appear if you have already pinch-zoomed to the highest possible magnification, and it does not offer any extra magnification if you pinch-zoom by smaller amount.

Find Similar Photos

You can search the thumbnails to find similar photos. This feature is still experimental. It can find photos with very obvious similarities in colors and textures, but it cannot recognize photos by theme. For example, it cannot recognize family or group shots, beach shots, sunsets, and so on.

The search feature is hidden. You can access it by double-tapping any photo. If iPhoto finds matches, it displays them in the preview area and plays a short repeating tone. If it cannot find matches, iPhoto plays a buzz.

Find Similar Photos

1 Open the thumbnail browser.

2 Double-tap any photo to begin the search.

iPhoto plays a short mechanical sound when it begins its search.

Ⓐ If there are matches, iPhoto plays a companion sound, and then highlights and displays matching photos in the preview area, just as if you selected them manually.

Note: "Similar" seems to mean "with similar colors." Shapes and composition are less important.

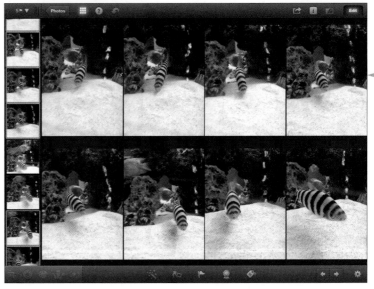

3 Double-tap a photo that does not match any others.

iPhoto plays the "searching" sound.

If there is no match, iPhoto plays the "no match found" buzz and does not show any further photos in the preview area.

TIPS

How fast is the search feature?
Searches are almost instant, although they can take a second or two if iPhoto is searching thousands of thumbnails. iPhoto plays a "searching now" tone when it begins. If you search a few hundred photos, the results appear almost immediately.

Can I tune the search to make it more sensitive or to recognize faces?
The search feature compares the range of colors in a photo. It does not recognize shapes. There are no search options, so you cannot fine-tune the search. iPhoto has no facial-recognition feature, and the search feature is not a substitute.

View Photo Information

You can use the Info option to display information about your photos, including the date of the photo, the camera used, and the camera settings. If your camera saves photos with location information, you can view the photo's location on a map and the approximate street address, if one exists.

The Info feature lists technical details including the aperture, shutter speed, lens focal length, exposure mode, exposure correction, and ISO number, known technically as EXIF (Exchangeable Image Format) data. You can also check the resolution in absolute dimensions and megapixels, the file size, and the file format.

View Photo Information

1 Open the thumbnail browser and tap a photo to select it.

2 Tap the info icon (⊡) to view information.

Ⓐ iPhoto displays the photo info in a pop-over, including the time, data, location, file type, and exposure mode.

Note: Not all photos include all possible information. If information is missing, boxes and fields are left empty.

Note: The exposure mode icon — the dot to the left of the JPEG box — uses standard symbols. For an explanation, see www.inspiredart.biz/Digital%20 Symbols.htm.

3 Tap the **Map** button to view the photo location.

Note: The Map button only appears when the photo includes location information.

iPhoto displays the photo location on a map with a red pin.

Ⓑ Optionally, you can drag the map in the frame to view more of it.

Note: You cannot pinch the map to zoom in and out.

④ Tap a different thumbnail to view that photo's info.

iPhoto displays the info for the new photo.

Note: You do not need to close the pop-over and reopen it to view the info for another photo.

⑤ Tap anywhere outside the Info pop-over to close it.

Note: You cannot select multiple photos while the pop-over is open.

Note: You can use the Comments button to add comments to photos uploaded to Facebook and Flickr as described in Chapter 12.

TIPS

Which iPhone and iPad models save location details?

All iPhones from the 3G onwards and all iPad 3G/4G models save location information as long as you enable location services in the Settings app. iPad Wi-Fi models use stored Wi-Fi information to estimate locations. Accuracy is very variable. If Wi-Fi is off, location services are also off.

Which digital cameras save location details?

The large number of models makes it impossible to list them. Many affordable cameras from around 2010 onwards include a *GPS* — Global Positioning Service — feature. GPS has been available as an option on professional cameras from around 2005. If in doubt, check your camera's manual to see if GPS is available.

CHAPTER 5

Organizing Photos

You can use albums and events to organize your photos. This chapter explains how you can create and delete albums and how to use them to manage your photos for sharing and viewing.

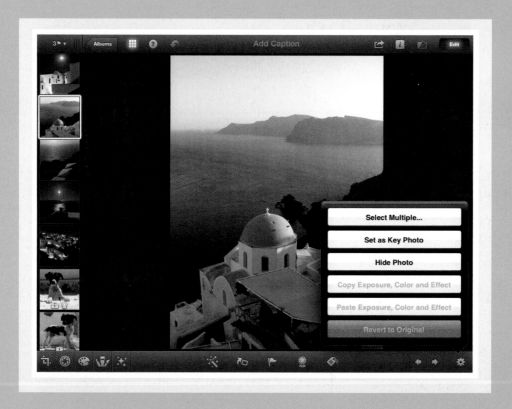

Understanding Albums and Events

You can use albums and events to organize your photos. Events group photos by date. Albums group photos by theme or subject. For example, you can create an album called "Family" to keep all your family photos together. iPhoto also creates a selection of smart albums automatically so you can view edited, beamed, flagged, tagged, or favorite photos together. iPhoto automatically creates a smart album for each *tag* — a word or description — you add to your photos. (For details see the next chapter.)

There is no other way to create albums or events in iPhoto. Typically you create albums in Photos for iOS, in iPhoto on the Mac, or with other Mac and PC software.

Understanding Albums

You can use albums to group related photos together for easy sharing or viewing. You can create as many albums as you want (until your device runs out of memory), but iPhoto lists all albums on a single page. One photo can be in multiple albums. To get the most from albums, use them selectively. Most users do not need more than a few tens of albums; if you create more, your albums can become difficult to manage. You can collect photos into albums using the Photos app on your device. You can also import albums created with iPhoto or

other software on a Mac or PC, such as Apple Aperture or Adobe Photoshop Elements. You cannot create this kind of album directly in iPhoto. But you can tag photos with simple descriptions such as wedding or vacation 2013. iPhoto automatically creates smart albums for photos that share a tag.

Understanding Events

Events are always imported. iPhoto on the Mac creates events automatically, grouping photos by date. iPhoto on iOS can also create events, but only if you upload photos to your device with the optional Camera Connection Kit. (See Chapter 2.) Unfortunately, photos in the camera roll are ignored. To create events from photos in the camera roll, upload them to iPhoto on a Mac and then re-import the events using iTunes.

Using iPhoto with Photos

Many of the features you might expect to find in iPhoto are available only in the Photos app included with every iOS device. For example, you can use the app to create, delete, and view albums, and to delete photos

from your device. If you create an album in Photos, iPhoto displays it on its Albums page. The camera roll, most albums, and all photos are shared between the apps. But the Photos app does not show the "smart" albums iPhoto creates for favorite, flagged, beamed, edited or tagged photos.

Using iPhoto for iOS with iPhoto for Mac

iPhoto for Mac offers more tools for managing photos, events, and albums and works well with iPhoto for iOS. iPhoto for Mac creates events automatically when you import photos from your device camera roll. You can also create albums and move photos between

events and albums. Note that iPhoto on the Mac cannot sync events or albums to a device. Instead, you use iTunes to pick the albums and events you want to view on your device and then use the sync feature to copy them. To delete albums from your device, deselect them in iTunes then sync.

Using Smart Albums

iPhoto automatically collects certain photos into albums which appear on the Albums page — Edited, Flagged, Beamed, Favorites, and the Camera Roll. These *smart albums* appear only when there is at least one qualifying photo. For example, the Edited album appears only after you edit a photo. These albums do not appear

in Photos, and you cannot delete them. You can view the photos in the albums in the usual way, by tapping the album on the Albums page and scrolling through the thumbnails. You can remove photos from these albums by hiding them or untagging them. (For details see the next chapter.)

View Albums

You can use the Albums page to view the albums on your device. iPhoto displays the albums on simulated glass shelves. If you have a lot of albums, iPhoto adds shelves for them automatically. You can drag your finger down the list to scroll through it.

The photo displayed on the cover of the album is called the *key photo*. Unless you tell it otherwise, iPhoto displays the first photo in the album, but you can pick any photo as the key photo. (For details, see the section "Set the Key Photo" later in this chapter.)

View Albums

① Launch iPhoto.

② Open the main page.

Note: If iPhoto launches in the thumbnail browser/editor, tap the return button near the top left to return to the main page. The label on the button varies, but its position on the screen is always the same.

③ If the albums are not visible, tap the **Albums** button to view a list of albums.

iPhoto displays the albums on your device with an attractive animation.

④ Drag the page up and down to view further albums.

⑤ Tap any album to open it.

Note: Smart albums, standard albums, and tag albums all have different border graphics.

iPhoto displays the photos in the album as a list of thumbnails.

Note: iPhoto remembers the last photo you select.

6 Drag the thumbnails up and down to view the complete list.

7 Tap any photo to select it and preview it.

iPhoto loads the photo into the preview area.

Note: You can now use the edit tools on the photo.

8 Swipe left and right to preview other photos in the album.

9 Tap the **Albums** button to return to the albums page.

Can I also view albums in the Photos app?
Photos and iPhoto share albums. When you download or create an album, you can view it in both apps. iPhoto's automatic albums — flagged, edited, favorite, and beamed photos — do not appear in Photos. Nor does the Photo Box album, but the Camera Roll album does as long as it holds at least one photo.

Can I change the order of the albums?
iPhoto sorts albums automatically into a "natural" near-alphabetic order. You cannot change this or sort the photos some other way. Even if you rearrange the album order in iPhoto on the Mac, iPhoto for iOS ignores that ordering.

Create an Album with Photos

Unfortunately, you cannot create albums in iPhoto. To create albums directly on your device, use the Photos app instead. After you create an album in Photos, it appears automatically in iPhoto, too. The two apps display albums in different ways — the Photos thumbnails list is much smaller and harder to see, and Photos has no key photo. Otherwise, albums are identical.

The Create Album option in Photos is not completely intuitive. It is also limited — you can add photos only to new albums, not to existing imported albums.

Create an Album with Photos

① Tap the **Photos** icon to launch Photos.

② Tap the **Albums** button to view albums.

Photos displays a list of albums.

③ Tap the **Edit** button to turn on album editing.

iPhoto turns on album editing. The Edit button is replaced with a Done button.

④ Tap the **New Album** button.

Note: The button is clearer when the alert is not visible.

⑤ Type a name for the album into the alert's text box.

⑥ Tap **Save** to create the new album.

Note: Tap **Cancel** if you change your mind. Photos returns to the Albums page and does not create the album.

7 Tap the photos you want to add to your new album.

iPhoto adds a check mark to a photo when you select it.

Note: Tap a photo again to deselect it.

8 Tap **Done** to add the photos to the new album.

Ⓐ iPhoto adds the photos to the new album and adds the album to the list.

Note: If you open iPhoto, you can see your new album there, too.

TIPS

How do I delete albums?

To delete an album, tap the **Edit** button and tap the close icon (❌) at the top left of the album. Tap **Done** when finished. You can only delete an album if you previously created it in Photos. You cannot delete albums you import with iTunes.

Is there a quick way to select multiple photos while I add them?

Unfortunately, there is no quick way to select a range of photos, but you can drag-select photos without tapping them one by one. Tap and hold two fingers on any photo. Drag both fingers slowly over the photos you want to select. Photos selects all the photos as your fingers move over them.

Set the Key Photo

You can set an album's *key photo* to select the photo that appears on its cover. You can use key photos for decoration, or to make the Albums page look more attractive. You can also use them to remind yourself of the contents of an album, or to display a favorite photo as the album cover.

Key photos have no other purpose. They are not pre-selected when you open an album, and there is no automatic album for key photos only. Key photos are not linked to iPhoto's Favorites feature, which is introduced in the next chapter.

Set the Key Photo

1 Launch iPhoto.

2 Open the main page.

3 If the albums are not visible, tap the **Albums** button.

iPhoto displays the albums.

4 Tap any new or imported album to open it.

Note: Key photos are not available in the Beamed, Edited, Flagged, or Favorite albums, or the camera roll.

⑤ Scroll through the thumbnails and tap your chosen key photo in the thumbnails list.

iPhoto previews the photo.

⑥ Tap the settings (gear) icon (⚙).

iPhoto displays a popover with various options.

⑦ Tap **Set as Key Photo** in the popover.

⑧ Tap the **Albums** button to return to the Albums list.

Ⓐ iPhoto displays the album with the new key photo on the cover.

Why does Photos ignore key photos?

Key photos are an iPhoto feature. Photos is a simpler app and does not support key photos. It displays a preview photo instead, which is usually the first photo in the album. The Camera Roll album is the exception. Both Photos and iPhoto display the most recent photo as the cover of the Camera Roll.

Can I set a key photo for the smart albums?

Smart albums do not support key photos. The cover photo is always the first photo added to the album.

Create Albums on a Mac

I f you have iPhoto for the Mac you can use it to create and manage albums. You can then import them into your device for viewing and sharing.

iPhoto on the Mac is easier to use than iPhoto for iOS because of the bigger screen and easy drag-and-drop photo management. You can get more from either application if you use them together. Creating and managing albums on a Mac is much more straightforward than managing them on a device.

Create Albums on a Mac

1 Launch iPhoto on your Mac.

Note: If you plug in a device, iPhoto launches automatically.

2 If you have new photos to import, click the **Import** button.

3 If you want iPhoto to create an event for each separate date as you import the photos, click **Split Events** (■ changes to ☑).

Note: If you do not click **Split Events**, iPhoto creates a single event for all the imported photos.

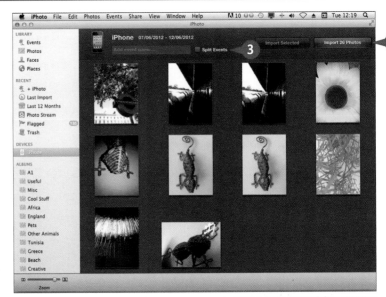

A After an import, iPhoto automatically selects the Last Import smart album.

4 To create a new album, click **File** and **New Album** or press ⌘+N.

Note: You can add any photo to any album. You do not have to import photos first.

96

iPhoto adds a new album named "untitled album" to the existing albums.

Note: iPhoto automatically adds all photos in the current thumbnails list to the new album.

⑤ Type a new name for your new album.

Note: Optionally, you can drag the album to a new position in the list after naming it.

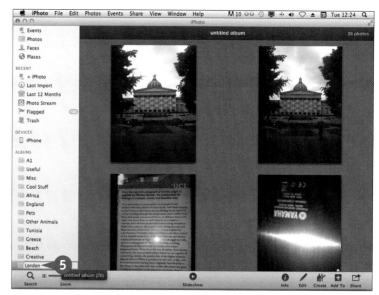

⑥ Drag a photo from any album, collection, or event and drop it on the new album.

iPhoto adds the photo to the album.

Note: iPhoto displays a floating translucent thumbnail of the photo as you drag it.

⑦ Repeat step **6** to add as many photos as you want from any collection or other album.

Note: You can delete a photo from an album by right-clicking it and selecting **Remove From Album**.

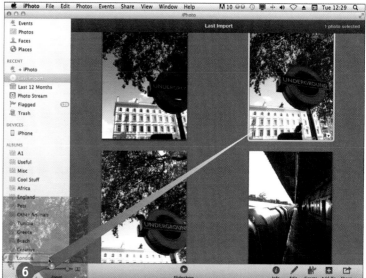

TIPS

Can I manage events in the same way?
Events are designed to organize photos by date, and iPhoto creates events automatically. But you can also add photos to events manually. Select the Photos library item to view a list of photos grouped into events. You can now drag any photo and drop it on any event, although if you have a lot of events, this may take a while.

Does iPhoto for iOS have the Faces and Places features?
The current version does not support face recognition and labeling. There is no single Places map of all photos, but you can view a photo's location in its info listing. For details, see the section "View Photo Information" in Chapter 4.

Import Albums and Events

After creating an album in iPhoto, you can use iTunes to import it to your device. You can also import events. The import feature turns your iPad or iPhone into a portable photo album. Photos in imported events and albums can also be edited with the advanced editing options in iPhoto for iOS.

The import feature in iTunes is easy to use, but it can also be easy to miss. You may want to practice it a few times.

Import Albums and Events

1. Plug your device into your Mac.

2. Launch iTunes if it does not launch automatically.

3. Select your device in the Devices list after it appears.

Note: If your device syncs automatically, wait until the sync ends.

4. Click **Photos**.

5. Click **Sync Photos from** (☐ changes to ☑).

6. Select **iPhoto** for syncing.

7. Click **Selected albums, Events, and Faces** (○ changes to ◉).

8. Select one of the date range options for events to include in the sync.

Note: Even if you select No Events, you can still choose events you want to include.

9 Click the albums you want to copy to your device (☐ changes to ☑).

10 Click the events you want to copy to your device (☐ changes to ☑).

11 Click the **Apply** button.

iPhoto copies the photos to the device. (This may take a few minutes.)

Note: If you uncheck an album or event that was previously copied, iTunes removes it from the device when it syncs.

12 Launch iPhoto on your device.

13 Select either **Albums** or **Events** on the main page.

Ⓐ iPhoto displays the albums or events you synced.

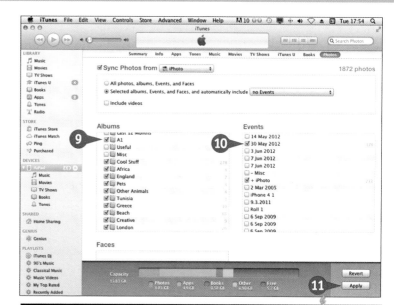

Can I sync all photos?

If you click **All photos, albums, Events, and Faces** in the Sync Photos box (○ changes to ◉), iTunes copies all photos to your device. Note that you may not want to do this, because it uses a lot of memory and can create an unmanageably large photo library on a device.

How do I sync from the Pictures folder instead of iPhoto?

Select the **Pictures** option in the Sync Photos From menu. Folders appear as albums. Be aware that syncing from Pictures on a Mac deletes all your iPhoto photos, and vice versa.

Clear the Camera Roll

Because of the album and event options, you may sometimes import photos from your device camera roll or dSLR memory card without deleting them automatically. If you do this you may eventually need to clear your camera roll or memory to remove the clutter.

You can re-import all photos into iPhoto to create a new event, but if you have already imported the photos this may create duplicates. A better option is to use the Image Capture utility to view and manage photos directly on your device.

Clear the Camera Roll

1 Launch Finder.

2 Find or navigate to your Applications folder.

3 Double-click the **Image Capture** application to launch it.

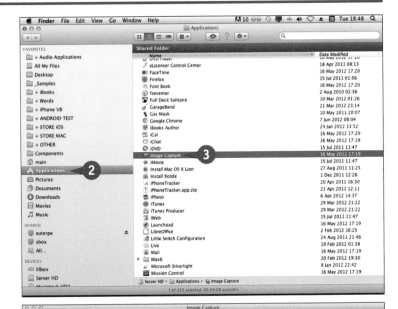

4 Select the **Other** option to import to a spare or new folder.

5 To create a new folder, click the **New Folder** button in the file sheet.

6 Type the name of the new folder in the dialog.

7 Click the **Create** button.

8 Click the **Choose** button in the file sheet.

Image Capture creates a new folder.

Note: You can also select an existing folder for the photos.

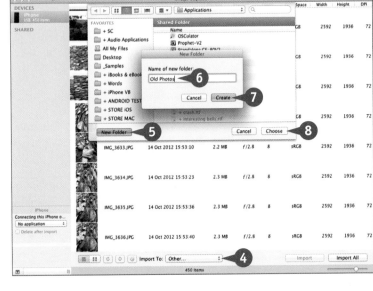

9 Select individual photos.

Note: You can click to select individual photos, or press and hold **Shift** and click two photos to select a range.

Note: You can skip step **8** if you want to delete all photos.

10 Click **Delete after import** (☐ changes to ☑).

11 Click **Import** to delete selected photos or **Import All** to delete all photos.

Note: Photos are imported to your Mac first and then deleted.

iPhoto deletes the photos from your device after copying them to the folder you selected.

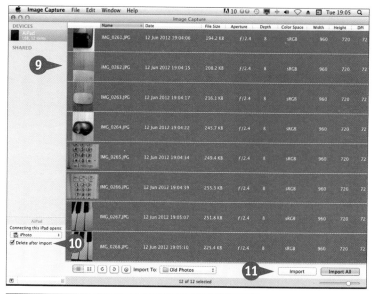

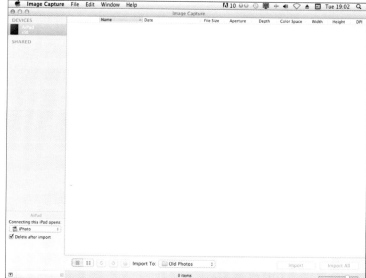

Can I delete hidden photos?
You can delete photos only from the camera roll. There is no way to delete photos in albums or events. Even if you use Photos, the trash can appears only for photos in the camera roll.

Can I delete photos using a PC instead of a Mac?
Your device appears automatically as a USB storage device when you plug it in. You can use Windows Explorer to select the device, open it, and delete the photos in the camera roll. There is no way to directly preview individual photos before you delete them.

CHAPTER 6

Tagging and Flagging Photos

You can use photo tagging to highlight the photos you love, to select photos for sharing, and to hide the photos you do not want to see. Tagging is easy, but learning to use tagging effectively takes some extra effort.

Understanding Photo Tagging

You can use tagging to select photos and organize them into special albums. iPhoto offers three standard tags you can apply manually to your photos: a flag to mark a photo temporarily, a favorite icon, and an X to hide a photo. You can also tag photos with words. iPhoto automatically applies a toolbox tag to photos after editing. And when you beam photos between devices, iPhoto marks them internally with yet another hidden tag.

The secret to using tagging efficiently is to understand how to use the different kinds of tags for common tasks, such as journal creation, smart album creation, and photo sharing.

Understanding Flagging

Use the flag tag to select photos for a task, such as sharing the photos to Facebook or adding them to a journal. Do not use flagging to mark photos you like. For speed, you can flag or unflag groups of photos with a few taps. You can also flag photos taken in the last day or last week. These more advanced flagging options are easy to miss, unless you know where to find them. Flagged photos appear automatically in the Flagged smart album.

Understanding Favorites

Use the blue ribbon tag to mark your favorite photos. iPhoto automatically collects favorite photos in a special Favorites smart album. As soon as you tag at least one photo as a favorite, the Favorites album is created for you and you can view it on the Albums page. Do not use the blue ribbon symbol to mark photos for sharing — use the flag instead.

Understanding Hidden Photos

Use the X tag to hide photos. Hiding photos does not delete them. (There is no way to delete photos in iPhoto.) It removes them from the main thumbnails list and all other photo collections. iPhoto includes an option to view all hidden photos, so you can change your mind and unhide them later. The hide feature is hidden in a popover.

Understanding Custom Tags

You can tag photos with your own words or phrases. For example, you can tag photos with the names of friends or family, or by subject or other content, or with a date or description of a special event. iPhoto automatically collects photos with the same tags into smart albums that appear in the Albums list. Note that tags only work on iDevices and are not copied when you sync your photos to a Mac or PC.

Understanding Edited Photos

When you edit a photo, iPhoto automatically tags it with a toolbox symbol. The symbol works much like a tag. You cannot apply it by hand, but you can use it as a quick way to select edited images for viewing or sharing. Edited photos automatically appear in the special Edited album.

Understanding Beamed Photos

When you share a photo with another device using iPhoto's beaming feature, iPhoto automatically applies a "beamed" tag. You cannot apply this tag manually, and it has no visible symbol. Beamed photos appear in the main Photos list and are collected automatically in the Beamed smart album. You cannot import beamed photos into iTunes or the Mac version of iPhoto.

Using Tags as Search Filters

You can use tags as a search filter. For example, the iPhoto thumbnails list can show photos that are tagged with a flag or marked as hidden. You can also view photos you have edited or list them by date. You can share a collection of photos tagged with a flag by beaming them, e-mailing them, or uploading them to a social networking site.

Using Flags for Viewing and Sharing

You can use combined tags to select photos for viewing or sharing. Begin by selecting photos manually, viewing an album, or filtering a collection in the thumbnail browser. Next, flag the photos using iPhoto's Flag All option. You can now share the photos or collect them into a journal. Use the Unflag All option to unflag them when done.

Flag Photos

You can flag photos in two ways. The thumbnail browser displays a list of tagging icons along the bottom toolbar. Tap the flag icon to flag a photo or unflag an already flagged photo.

There is also a quick but hidden way to flag multiple photos. Select one or more photos, and then tap the flag icon and hold it. iPhoto displays a popover with further options. You can use this feature to flag photos in groups, or to unflag photos with a single tap. These group options work only on the currently visible thumbnails.

Flag Photos

1 Launch iPhoto.

2 Open the thumbnail browser from within an album, an event, or the general photos collection.

3 Tap the **Edit** button at the top right if edit mode is not selected, and then tap any thumbnail to select it for viewing.

Note: The steps in this section also work if you select a group of photos.

The thumbnail browser displays the photo.

4 Tap the flag icon (⚑) to flag the photo.

iPhoto flashes a brief animation of a flag, adds the flag symbol to the photo, and also highlights the flag icon in the toolbar.

5 Tap the flag icon (⚑) again to unflag the photo.

iPhoto displays the flag disappearing to the right, removes the flag symbol from the photo, and unhighlights the flag on the toolbar.

Note: Flag symbols on photos appear in the thumbnail view in the editor, but not in the Photos collection.

6 Tap and hold the flag icon (📌).

iPhoto displays a popover with further options.

7 Tap one of the options to flag a group of photos.

Note: The 24 hours or 7 days options flag photos taken in those periods, as well as any undated photos.

8 Tap **Choose Photos** to select multiple photos or a range of photos.

iPhoto flags the selected photos in a group.

9 Tap **Unflag All** to unflag a group of photos.

Note: This option unflags all photos visible in the current thumbnails. It does not unflag other photos.

TIPS

Why do the Flag All and Unflag All options appear only in some albums?

There is no official explanation, but experiments suggest that the Flag All and Unflag All options appear in albums created with photos taken on an iPhone or iPad. The options are missing on albums created with photos taken with any other digital cameras.

Is there a quick way to unflag all photos?

Keep in mind that the Unflag All option unflags only the photos visible in the current thumbnails list, not all the flagged photos on your device. To unflag all photos on your device, open the Flagged album, tap and hold the flag icon (📌), and then tap **Unflag All**.

Create Favorites

You can tag photos as favorites. Tagging a photo as a favorite marks it with a rosette icon and automatically adds it to iPhoto's Favorites album.

The Favorites feature is limited. You cannot share favorite photos directly or use favorites as a filter for thumbnails. But you can open the Favorites album, flag every photo in it, and then share the flagged photos.

Create Favorites

1 Launch iPhoto.

2 Open any album, event, or the photo list.

3 Tap the **Edit** button at the top right if edit mode is not selected, and then tap any thumbnail to select it for viewing.

Note: The steps in this section also work if you select a group of photos.

The thumbnail browser displays the photo.

4 Tap the favorite icon (■) to favorite the photo.

iPhoto flashes a brief animation of a rosette, adds the favorite symbol to the photo, and highlights the favorite icon in the toolbar.

5 Tap the favorite icon (■) again to unfavorite the photo.

iPhoto shows the rosette disappearing to the right, removes the small favorite symbol from the photo, and unhighlights the favorite icon on the toolbar.

6 Return to the Albums page to view iPhoto's albums.

7 Tap the Favorites album to open it.

Note: You must have at least one favorite photo to see this album.

iPhoto opens the album and displays your favorite photos.

8 Tap the **Albums** button to return to the main thumbnails list.

TIPS

Can I flag and favorite the same photo?
You can flag any photo, so you can flag and favorite the same photo. However, you cannot hide and favorite a photo at the same time. Hiding a photo unfavorites it — and vice versa.

Why do photos disappear from the Favorites album when I unfavorite them?
The Favorites album displays only photos with the favorites tag. If you remove the tag, the photo immediately disappears from the album. This makes sense in theory, but can be distracting in practice. To show the photo again, tap the undo icon (■) in the top toolbar.

Add Custom Tags

You can add custom tags of your own words or phrases to your photos. Photos that share custom tags appear automatically in their own smart albums on the Albums page. You can also search for custom tags when you view photos.

The custom tag feature is easy to use but very powerful. For speed and convenience you can use the multiple selection features introduced in Chapter 4 to add a custom tag to many photos at once. You can create as many custom tags as you want, but too many tags can clutter the album page and search list.

Add Custom Tags

1 Launch iPhoto.

2 Open any album, event, or the photo list.

3 Tap the **Edit** button at the top right if edit mode is not selected, and then tap any thumbnail to select it for viewing.

Note: The steps in this section also work if you select a group of photos.

The thumbnail browser displays the photo.

4 Tap and hold the custom tag icon ( ).

A iPhoto displays a tag popover. If you have already created custom tags they appear in this list.

Note: This example shows two tags created earlier, Flowers and Garden.

5 Tap one of the tags to apply it to the photo.

B iPhoto flashes a brief tag animation and applies the tag to the photo.

Note: You can apply more than one tag to a photo.

6 Tap the text box at the top of the popover to create a new custom tag.

7 When the keyboard appears, type your new tag into the box.

8 Tap **Done** or **Hide Keyboard** when finished.

iPhoto saves the new tag to the tag list, applies it to the photo, and hides the keyboard.

9 Tap the **Albums**, **Events**, or **Photos** button to the return to iPhoto's main page.

10 Tap the **Albums** button to view the albums if they are not already visible.

C Every tag automatically creates a smart album in the album list. iPhoto displays a smart album for the photos tagged with every custom tag you create.

Note: The tagged smart albums appear with a wallet/pocket graphic to remind you they are not like iPhoto's other albums.

TIPS

Can I delete a tag from the list?
You can only delete tags if no photos use them. To deselect all photos, use the multiple selection options introduced in Chapter 4 and use the tag popover to remove the tags. Tap the **Edit** button at the top right of the popover. Tap the red minus sign and the delete button to delete a tag. You can also use edit mode to change the order of the tags by dragging them up and down the list.

Is there a quicker way to tag photos?
When the popover is open, tap any tag in the column at the right. iPhoto selects a tag and displays a single gray tag icon in that column. Tap anywhere to close the popover. You can now select any photo or photos in the usual way and tag them with the tag you selected by tapping the custom tag icon (🔳).

Hide Photos

You can use the hide tag in iPhoto to hide photos you do not like. Hiding a photo makes it disappear from the main photo list and from any albums and events that feature it. It also makes the photo disappear from the Camera Roll album in iPhoto.

However, hiding a photo does not delete the photo from your device. You can still see the photo in the Photos app and in any journals you added it to. Unlike iPhoto's other tagging features, the Hide option is in a popover.

Hide Photos

1 Launch iPhoto.

2 Open the thumbnail browser from within an album, an event, or the general photos collection.

3 Tap the **Edit** button at the top right if edit mode is not selected, and then tap any thumbnail to select it for viewing.

Note: The steps in this section also work if you select a group of photos.

The thumbnail browser displays the photo.

4 Tap the settings (gear) icon (⚙) to display a popover.

5 Tap **Hide Photo**.

A iPhoto flashes a red cross and hides the photo.

6 Tap the disclosure triangle at the top of the thumbnails.

iPhoto displays a popover with tag-related search and sort options.

7 Tap **Hidden Items** to view the hidden photos in the currently selected album or event.

Note: To see all hidden photos on your device, select the Photos collection first and then open the popover and tap **Hidden Items**.

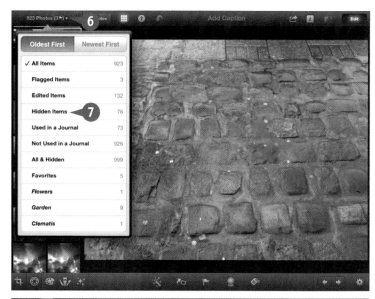

iPhoto displays the hidden photos in the current album, event, or photo list.

8 Tap any photo to select it.

9 Tap the settings (gear) icon (▓) to show the popover.

10 Tap **Unhide Photo** to unhide the photo.

Note: Unhiding a photo removes it from the hidden thumbnails list. The photo reappears in its original location.

TIPS

Why is there no way to delete photos?
iPhoto does not duplicate features available elsewhere. Because you can delete photos in the Photos app, Apple apparently decided there was no need to include a delete option in iPhoto.

Is there a quick way to bulk delete a group of unwanted photos?
Only from the camera roll. On a Mac, you can use the Image Capture application to bulk delete photos. On a PC, you can connect the device over USB and delete files manually in Windows Explorer. For details, see Chapter 5. There is no easy way to bulk delete photos without a Mac or PC.

Search Tagged Photos

You can view tagged photos in two ways. Edited, Tagged, Beamed, and Favorite photos are automatically collected into albums. To view these photos, open their smart albums on the Albums page, as described earlier in this chapter.

When you are viewing any album or event or the photos list in the editor, you can use a popover to view only Flagged, Edited, or Hidden photos; photos with custom tags; and photos used, or not used, in journals. The popover includes a search order option so you view your selection in forward or reverse date order.

Search Tagged Photos

1 Launch iPhoto.

2 Open the thumbnail browser from within an album, an event, or the general photos collection.

3 Tap the disclosure triangle at the top of the thumbnail browser.

A iPhoto displays a popover with various search options for the thumbnails.

Note: The totals at the right show the number of each type of item.

4 Tap any option to view the matching photos.

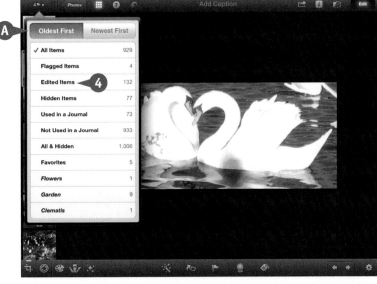

iPhoto displays only the photos with the tag you select from the current album, event, or collection.

Note: The example is showing edited photos. Note the toolbox symbol on every photo.

5 Tap any photo to view it.

Note: You can select and view multiple photos in the usual ways.

6 Tap **Oldest First** or **Newest First** to show the oldest or newest thumbnails at the top of the list.

B iPhoto changes the date order in the thumbnails list.

TIPS

Why are some photos missing when I view all hidden photos on my device?

Because they have been deleted manually in the Photos app or using a Mac or PC. iPhoto keeps a "slot" for every photo it shows. Empty slots remain after photos are deleted. iPhoto displays them as gray squares.

Why is there no way to select favorite photos in the popover?

This would be a useful option, but Apple has not included it. To view favorite photos, open the Favorites album. Unfortunately, there is no way to view only your favorite photos in an album or event.

Caption Photos

You can add short descriptive captions to your photos. A caption appears as a line of text above a selected photo, and is added to thumbnails rather like a tag. But captions are purely for decoration and description. You cannot search your photos for a caption.

When you add a photo to a journal, its caption appears on the photo automatically.

Caption Photos

1 Launch iPhoto.

2 Open the thumbnail browser from within an album, an event, or the general photos collection.

3 Tap the **Edit** button at the top right if edit mode is not selected, and then tap any thumbnail to select it for viewing.

4 Tap **Add a Caption** above the photo.

Note: The text lacks contrast and is easy to miss.

iPhoto shows the keyboard and a blank caption ready for editing.

5 Use the keyboard to type text into the caption.

Note: Text is auto-corrected as you type.

6 Tap **Done** when finished.

(A) iPhoto adds the caption to the photo's title bar and thumbnail.

(7) Add more captions and select the thumbnail of a different captioned photo.

(B) iPhoto displays the new photo's caption in the title bar.

(8) Add a captioned photo to a journal (see Chapter 13) and open the journal.

iPhoto automatically displays the caption in the journal.

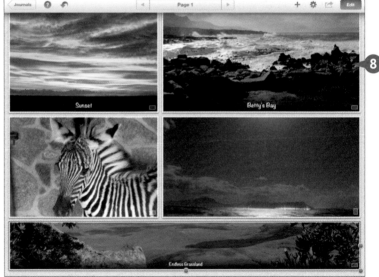

TIPS

Are captions visible in iPhoto for the Mac?
No. When you add a caption to a photo in iPhoto in iOS and import it to iPhoto on the Mac, the caption does not appear on the Mac. The description remains blank. This may — perhaps — be fixed in a future version of iPhoto for the Mac.

Is there a limit to the length of a caption?
Captions always appear on a single line. You can make the text as long as you want, but iPhoto displays only a short section of around 30 characters. If the text is very long, iPhoto automatically shrinks the font to make more of the text visible. Very long captions are still cut off.

CHAPTER 7

Getting Started with Editing

You can use iPhoto's editing tools to correct and improve your photos. There is a lot to learn about editing. This chapter introduces iPhoto's simplest tools for very basic edits, which include cropping, rotating, and enhancing a photo. The next few chapters introduce further enhancement tools for more subtle and powerful corrections and creative applications.

Learn about Editing

You can use iPhoto's editing tools in two ways. You can apply simple corrections — for example, you can rotate a photo slightly to fix a slanted horizon. You can also crop a photo to remove features that distract from the person or scene you want a viewer to concentrate on. More complex corrections can improve the look and feel of a photo by changing the lighting, contrast, color, or exposure.

Most photos can be improved or enhanced. This chapter introduces iPhoto's simplest editing tools. The following chapters introduce tools you can use to create more complex effects.

Understanding Auto-Enhance

You can use auto-enhance to improve the color and contrast in a photo. Auto-enhance is a "magic" single-click option with no settings. Technically, it increases the saturation and contrast in an image. If your photo has good saturation and contrast already, this tool does very little — in fact, you may not be able to tell the difference between the enhanced photo and the original. On most photos the effect is more obvious, but still subtle. You can use it as a good starting point before you add further edits.

Understanding Rotation

iPhoto includes two rotation tools. The first tool spins a photo in 90-degree steps. You can use this tool to correct photos that were taken upside down or with the camera on its side. The second tool is combined with the cropping tool. You can use it to fix slanted horizons, or to rotate photos for more creative reasons — for example, some photos do not have a clear horizontal marker, and look better when rotated slightly. The second tool always crops some of the detail at the edges of a photo to hide the empty areas that a rotation creates.

Understanding Cropping

The crop tool removes the edges around a photo. You can use cropping to change the relative height and width — the *aspect ratio* — of a photo to match the standard dimensions used for cards, prints, or posters. You can also crop a photo to a square frame, which is a popular option for web pages. Creatively you can use cropping to remove clutter and irrelevant detail

around the edges of a photo to highlight the most important features. Cropping literally chops away the sides of a photo, so it always creates a smaller photo with a lower resolution. For best results start with the highest resolution you can. Otherwise you may be left with a tiny image too small to be printed.

Understanding Versions in iPhoto

Whenever you edit a photo, iPhoto keeps the original. You can use a compare tool to preview the original and edited versions. If you do not like your edits, iPhoto includes a Revert to Original option, which throws away your edits and restores the original. You can re-edit and restore a photo as many times as you want until you create an edited version you are happy with. No

easy way exists to compare different edited versions within iPhoto itself. However, you can share both original and any edited versions to your camera roll. You can then review them, save them to a Mac or some other device, or edit them further.

Understanding Undo and Redo

When you revert to an original photo, you lose all edits. iPhoto includes an undo feature. You can use it to compare a photo before and after an edit and step back through a series of edits. If you do not like your edit, you can cancel it. You can also redo an edit to repeat it after undoing it, which is a good way to compare before and after views.

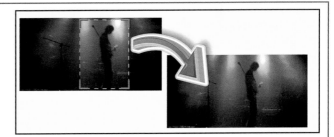

Using Auto-Enhance

Auto-enhance is a simple one-click photo improvement tool. You can use it to make colors brighter and more attractive, and to improve contrast.

Auto-enhance has no settings and you cannot control what it does. You either apply it or not. Although the effect is simple, it improves most photos, and works reliably on portraits. The results on more complex or abstract shots are less predictable, but usually worth trying.

Using Auto-Enhance

1 Launch iPhoto.

2 Open the thumbnail browser.

3 Tap any thumbnail to select a photo for enhancement.

4 If the bottom toolbar is not visible, tap the **Edit** button.

iPhoto highlights the Edit button in blue and displays the bottom toolbar.

5 Tap the **Auto-Enhance** icon (![icon]).

A iPhoto starts applying the effect. (Wait until the alert disappears.)

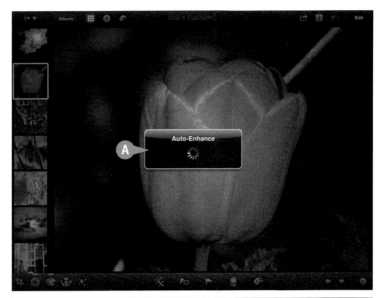

iPhoto enhances the colors in the original photo.

B iPhoto highlights the tools it applied.

Note: The effect is subtle. The changes are more obvious on the third-generation and later iPads because they have a better color display.

TIPS

What does auto-enhance really do?
The details are an Apple secret, but auto-enhance increases color saturation — that is, it makes colors brighter and more intense. As a useful side effect this also improves the contrast.

Can I apply auto-enhance more than once?
No. Auto-enhance is designed to create a subtle, natural-looking improvement. You cannot use it to create garish colors. The first time you apply it, it increases color as much as it can. Applying it again does nothing. If you want to create more dramatic color edits, use the tools introduced in Chapter 8.

Fix a Sideways or Inverted Photo

Sometimes you may need to take a photo with an iPhone on its side or upside down. Occasionally you may forget which way is up.

iPhoto includes a simple quick-fix option for inverted photos. You can rotate a photo by 90 degrees by tapping the rotation tool, or by spinning the photo with two fingers. The rotation tool includes a hidden feature — if you tap and hold it, you can choose the rotation direction.

Fix a Sideways or Inverted Photo

1 Launch iPhoto.

2 Open the thumbnail browser.

3 Tap any thumbnail to select a photo for enhancement.

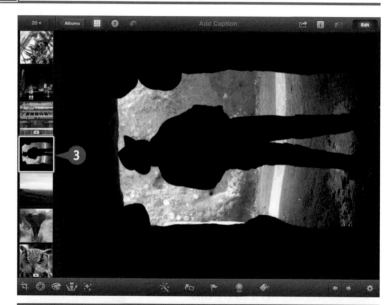

4 Tap the **Rotation** icon (   ).

A iPhoto rotates the photo 90 degrees to the right (clockwise).

B iPhoto adds the toolbox marker to the photo's thumbnail to show it has been edited.

⑤ Tap and hold the **Rotation** icon (▣).

iPhoto displays a popover with options to rotate the photo clockwise or counterclockwise.

⑥ Tap the counterclockwise option to rotate the photo to the left.

⑦ Tap the clockwise option to rotate the photo to the right.

⑧ Place two fingers on the photo.

⑨ Rotate them to spin the photo.

iPhoto "snaps" the rotation to the nearest 90 degrees — that is, you can only rotate a photo to the next whole side, and not by a smaller amount.

Note: Two-finger rotation is slightly tricky, so you may need to try this gesture a few times before it works for you.

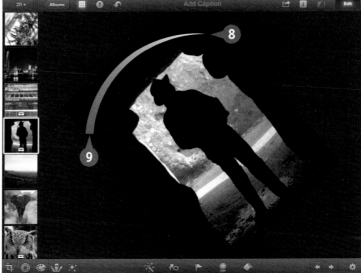

TIPS

Does a rotation count as a permanent edit?
Spinning a photo with your fingers or with the photo rotation tool is a permanent edit. iPhoto marks the photo thumbnail with its toolbox marker, and the photo appears in the Edited smart album.

Does rotating a photo affect the image quality?
Rotation is not an exact science, and if you rotate a photo over and over the quality will eventually degrade. But you would need to repeat a rotation tens or even hundreds of times to see an obvious difference. So in practice, rotation has no effect.

125

Fix the Horizon

Many photographers, including professionals, find it difficult to take photos with a perfectly level horizon. iPhoto includes a quick-fix tool for obviously skewed photos. The tool is very easy to use — you can fix a horizon with two taps.

The tool is not infallible. It may miss a horizon that is obvious to a human viewer, or make a mistake in its estimate. You can fine-tune the rotation before applying it. You can also set it manually, as described in the next section.

Fix the Horizon

1 Launch iPhoto.

2 Open the thumbnail browser.

3 Tap the thumbnail of a photo with a skewed horizon.

4 Tap the **Crop** icon (⬚).

A If iPhoto can find a horizon, it displays an anchor point X and an arrow, joined by a line that estimates the angle of the horizon.

5 Tap the arrow to fix the horizon.

Note: You can tap the X icon opposite the arrow to cancel.

iPhoto rotates the photo to fix the horizon.

6 Drag the rotation control to fine-tune the rotation.

Note: You can use the grid as a reference.

7 Tap the **Crop** icon (⬚) again to repair and set the horizon.

Can I force iPhoto to find a horizon?
If iPhoto cannot find a horizon, the anchor point X and arrow do not appear. You cannot force iPhoto to display them. If you can see the horizon but iPhoto cannot, you can rotate the photo manually to fix it.

If the horizon looks straight on the grid, why does my photo still look skewed?
Some camera and lens combinations cannot produce a straight horizon. For example, if you use a wide-angle lens, the horizon may be curved. In some photos, vertical lines may not be at right angles to the horizontal lines on the grid — for example, the sides of tall buildings may be angled because of perspective. iPhoto does not include tools to fix these advanced problems.

Rotate a Photo Manually

You can rotate a photo's horizon manually or for creative effects. The rotation feature is built into the crop tool, but they are somewhat independent. You can crop a photo without rotating it, but for practical reasons rotating a photo always crops the edges.

Rotation is limited to 20 degrees left or right. You can use a rotation dial to set it very accurately. A grid appears automatically to help you align features in the photo. You can also tilt your device to control the rotation. This is called *gyro-rotation*. It is a clever feature, but can be tricky to control.

Rotate a Photo Manually

1 Launch iPhoto.

2 Open the thumbnail browser.

3 Tap the thumbnail of a photo to select it for rotation.

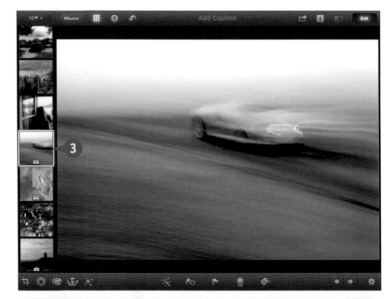

4 Tap the **Crop** icon (▣).

A iPhoto displays the rotation dial.

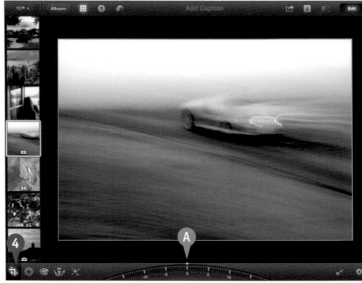

5 Drag the dial left or right to rotate the photo.

B You can tap the dial to use gyro-rotation.

Note: When gyro-rotation is enabled, iPhoto outlines the dial in blue.

Note: Keep your device flat and rotate it horizontally to set the amount of gyro-rotation. Do not tilt it vertically.

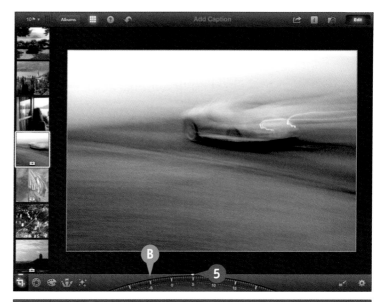

6 Touch the photo with two fingers and spin them to rotate the photo.

Note: iPhoto displays a reference grid as you rotate the photo. It also displays the uncropped edges of the photo around the visible area.

7 Drag the cropped area to center it.

Note: You can also resize it with a pinch zoom. You can zoom in or out.

8 Tap the **Crop** icon () again to finish the rotation.

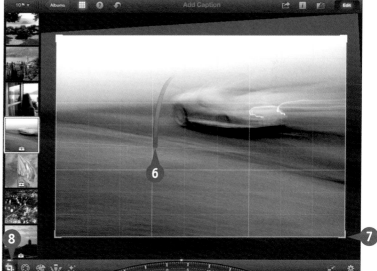

TIPS

Why does rotating a photo always crop the edges?

If you rotate a photo without cropping it, it loses triangular "wedges" on each side. iPhoto resizes photos automatically to avoid this. You can use a pinch zoom to resize the photo manually if iPhoto is cropping too much, or too little, of the photo.

Why is the rotation limited to twenty degrees?
The rotation option is designed for corrections, not for creative effects. It would be useful to have a wider range, but unfortunately this option is not available.

Crop a Photo

You can use cropping to prepare a photo for printing. For example, in the United States, small photo prints have standard sizes in inches — 4 × 6, 5 × 7, and so on. Many cameras produce prints that do not match these sizes exactly. You can use the crop tool to chop away the sides of a photo to make it fit a standard print size. iPhoto includes a selection of standard crop ratios. For creative applications, you can create your own ratio, or use cropping to highlight an area by removing unwanted features in a photo.

Crop a Photo

1 Launch iPhoto.

2 Open the thumbnail browser.

3 Tap the thumbnail of a photo to select it for rotation.

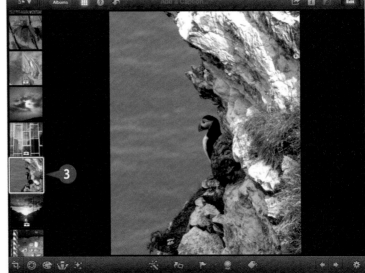

4 Tap the **Crop** icon (⬚).

5 Tap and drag the corner and/or edges of a photo to change the crop.

Note: You can repeat step **5** until the crop looks good.

Ⓐ You can tap the **Lock Aspect Ratio** icon (⬚) to lock the ratio before cropping.

Note: This example does not show a locked ratio.

6 Use a two-finger pinch to zoom or expand the area within the crop.

Note: You can also drag the image within the frame to reposition it.

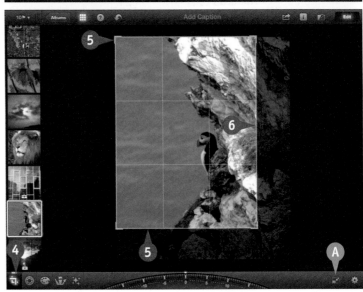

130

7 To select a standard crop ratio, tap the settings (gear) icon (⚙).

8 Tap one of the standard crop ratios to select it.

iPhoto immediately resizes the crop frame around the photo.

9 Tap the dot selector to see a further page of preset ratios.

Note: After selecting a ratio, you can drag and zoom the photo within the crop frame to improve the composition.

B You can drag the rotation dial to rotate the photo within the crop frame.

C iPhoto shows a preview of the cropped photo.

10 Tap the **Crop** icon (▣) again to finish cropping.

iPhoto applies the crop and adds a toolbox edit marker to the photo's thumbnail.

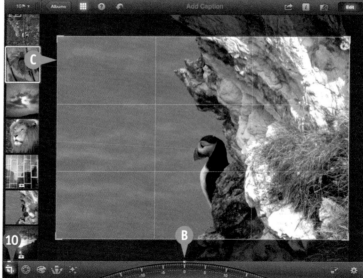

TIPS

How do I know which ratio to select?
Many of the ratios match standard print sizes, such as 5 × 7 inches. For others, divide the print size down until it is as small as it can be, and use that as the ratio. For example, 6 × 8 inches is the same as 3 × 4 — you can divide each number by two.

Can I crop too much?
If you take a distant photo of someone and use the pinch zoom feature to crop the photo around them and zoom it at the same time, you get a fuzzy result. You can tell you have cropped too much when a photo loses sharpness. Fuzziness can look fine on the screen, but is less appealing when printed.

View Edited and Unedited Photos

You can use the Show Original feature in iPhoto to compare an edited photo with the unedited original. You can also use a feature called Revert to Original to cancel all edits. Both features work with multiple edits, including the simple edits described in this chapter, and the more complex editing features introduced later in this book.

When you compare versions, iPhoto always displays the photo as it was taken or uploaded. The edited version shows every change you made to it. When you revert to original, all your edits are lost and you can start again from scratch.

View Edited and Unedited Photos

1 Launch iPhoto.

2 Open the thumbnail browser.

3 Tap the thumbnail of any edited photo to select it for comparison.

A iPhoto displays the edited photo in the preview area.

4 Tap the **Show Original** icon (▨) to show the original unedited photo.

B iPhoto displays the original photo.

5 Tap the **Show Original** icon (▨) again to swap back the edited version.

6 Tap the settings (gear) icon (⚙).

iPhoto displays extra options in a popover.

7 Tap the **Revert to Original** option.

Note: If you do not see the Revert to Original option, tap the **Edit** button at the top right twice.

ⓒ iPhoto cancels all edits, displays the original photo, and removes the toolbox marker from the photo thumbnail.

Note: You can revert at any time, even after you preview other photos, potentially months or years after you finish editing.

TIPS

Can iPhoto show the original and edited versions at the same time?

No. You can view an edited photo or an original photo. One always replaces the other. However, you can share any photo to the camera roll to create a fresh independent copy at any time.

Can I revert and change my mind?

If you revert to original and tap the undo icon (↺) — described in the next section — iPhoto restores the original edits. You can use this option if you change your mind and decide you want to keep the edits after all. For quick comparisons, use the Show Original icon (▨) instead.

Using Undo and Redo

iPhoto saves a copy of your changes as you edit. You can then use the undo icon to step back through your edits, either to correct a mistake or to compare each change with the edits around it.

This means iPhoto supports multiple levels of undo. It also includes a feature called redo. After you undo edits you can step forward through them, repeating each edit you made originally. These are powerful options. You can use them to review changes as you work, correcting mistakes and keeping the changes that look good.

Using Undo and Redo

1 Launch iPhoto.

2 Open the thumbnail browser.

3 Tap the thumbnail of any photo for editing.

4 Edit the photo.

Note: You can use any of the editing features in this chapter or the following chapters.

5 Tap the undo icon (◼) to undo the last edit.

iPhoto undoes the last edit and displays the photo as it was before you changed it.

6 Tap the undo icon (◼) repeatedly.

iPhoto undoes your edits one by one, stepping back through them and showing the photo as it was before each change.

7 Tap and hold the undo icon (◼).

iPhoto displays a popover with undo and redo options.

8 Tap the **Redo** option.

Note: iPhoto displays the name of each operation in the popover.

iPhoto redoes the edit.

Note: The popover stays visible after each operation. You can move in either direction through the undo list by tapping the undo or redo options as they appear.

TIPS

How many levels of undo are there?
Apple does not specify a limit. In practice, there seem to be many tens of steps, so you are unlikely to run out of steps if you use this feature. However, if memory is tight, iPhoto may run out of memory and crash. Note also that when you work on another photo, iPhoto forgets the first photo's undo history.

What happens if I start editing midway through the undo list?
iPhoto throws away all subsequent edits in the list and keeps your new changes. You can still step back to the start of the undo list, but you can no longer step forward through your original edits. However, you can step forward through the new changes you make.

CHAPTER 8

Correcting and Enhancing Photos

You can use iPhoto's editing tools to fix mistakes in lighting, color, and contrast and to adjust photos to make them look better.

Learn about Enhancement

The previous chapter introduced the crop tool and the auto-enhance tool. This chapter introduces the color and exposure tools. You can use these two tools to improve most photos by correcting and enhancing color and by changing the brightness and contrast.

After you enhance your photos, you can use the creative tools introduced in later chapters to make further changes or fix more specific problems.

Understanding Enhancement

Cameras always lie, because a photo always captures one of many possible views of a scene. A photo of a person shot outdoors at midday looks very different from a photo taken near sunset, or under cloud, or indoors. You can use enhancements to compensate for some of these distortions — for example, to remove the yellow coloring added to scenes lit by

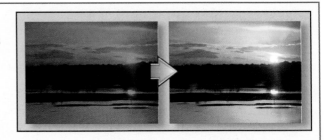

candles or incandescent bulbs. You can also use enhancements to change the mood of a photo in more creative ways, making it lighter or darker, and the colors more or less vivid and accurate. Like all edits in iPhoto, enhancements are *nondestructive*; you can always remove them to restore the original photo.

Understanding Exposure

Cameras work by measuring the light in a scene. For good results, a camera has to make a good estimate of the average brightness — the *exposure* — of a scene. Cameras do not always get this right. Semi-pro cameras have complicated exposure options. They work well with practice, but it can take beginners a while to master them. Budget

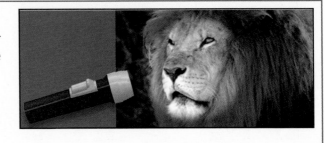

pocket cameras usually guess the exposure correctly when the light is good, but may struggle when there is too little light, or too much light. You can use iPhoto's Exposure tool to correct both kinds of errors.

Understanding Color

Color has a big impact on the mood of an image. Bright, bold colors can make a photo more appealing. Alternatively, you may want to tone down the color in a scene for special effects. iPhoto's Color tool gives you both options. You can make the colors in a photo stronger or less vibrant. You can control the red, green, and blue shades

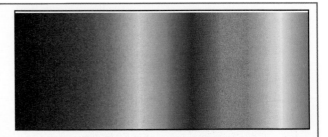

separately for extra control. For example, you can make a blue sky more vibrant without changing the other parts of a scene.

Understanding White Balance

Most people do not notice the difference in color between indoor and outdoor lighting until they take a photo indoors and wonder why it looks so yellow. Your eyes compensate automatically for different types of lighting. Most cameras try to compensate too, using *white balance*, a process that tries to re-create the true colors however a scene is lit.

iPhoto includes a white balance tool for fixing color errors, with various presets for common lighting types. You can also use a manual white balance option to try to fix the colors by hand.

Understanding Two-Axis Control

The enhancement tools have a unique editing option. If you tap and hold a finger on a photo, iPhoto displays four arrows. Moving your finger in the direction of each arrow changes the image in a different way. iPhoto labels the arrows so you can see what they do without having to look up the details in the help. This two-axis, one-finger editing gives you a quick and intuitive way to improve your photos.

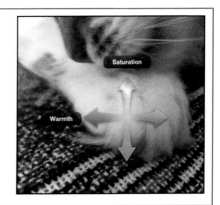

Understanding the Limitations of Enhancement

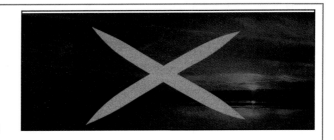

You can use enhancements for simple corrections and for more extreme creative effects, but the enhancement tools cannot perform miracles. You cannot correct the exposure of a completely dark photo taken with too little light, or a photo that is so bright all the detail has been washed out. You cannot add colors to a scene that does not have them — for example, a snow field under heavy cloud does not have much color. The enhancement tools can work only with the detail you give them. You cannot fix very bad photos that should be taken again.

Control Enhancements by Dragging

You can control the color and enhancement tools with a selection of on-screen sliders. But both tools also include a hidden one-finger drag option that can change two settings at once.

To use this feature, select the Color or Enhancement tool and tap and hold anywhere on the photo. iPhoto displays four arrows, although a few options display two — one up, and one down. Keep your finger on the screen and drag it to make changes. The controls are *contextual* — iPhoto tries to guess what you are doing and displays the controls it thinks you need.

Control Enhancements by Dragging

1 Launch iPhoto and open the editor.

2 Tap a thumbnail to select it for editing.

3 If the Edit button is not selected, tap it to enter edit mode.

4 Tap the **Exposure** icon (⬛).

5 Tap and hold a finger in the preview area.

A iPhoto displays four arrows.

6 Drag your finger up and down to set brightness.

7 Drag your finger left and right to set contrast.

B iPhoto moves the main controls automatically as you drag your finger.

⑧ Tap the **Color** icon (🎨).

⑨ Tap and hold a finger in the preview area.

Ⓒ iPhoto displays two or four arrows.

Note: The up/down Saturation arrow always appears.

Note: The left/right arrow displays Warmth, Blue Skies, or Greenery depending whether you tap a red/orange, blue, or green part of the image.

Note: If iPhoto does not recognize a color when you tap, the left/right arrow does not appear at all.

⑩ Drag your finger up and down and left and right to change the color.

TIPS

Does this feature appear elsewhere in iPhoto?
The arrows appear only in the color and exposure editors. The other editors and tools have different controls.

Can I force iPhoto to work with a color?
In the color editor, iPhoto picks the left/right arrow options from the color you tap. If you want to change one of the other colors, you can use the sliders in the usual way. For more information, see the section "Work with Different Colors" later in this chapter.

Understanding Exposure

When a photo's exposure is correct, it has a good balance between highlights and shadows. The lightest and darkest areas of the scene reveal as much detail as possible. An *overexposed* photo looks washed out, with no detail in the highlights. An *underexposed* photo appears murky and dark, with no detail in the shadows.

iPhoto includes an Exposure tool. You can use the tool to repair photos with poor exposure. You can also use it to experiment with the brightness, contrast, and dark/light balance in a photo. This can change the mood in a creative way and enhance the visual impact.

Understanding Exposure

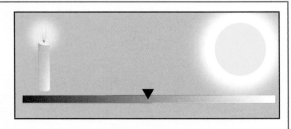

Digital cameras measure the light from each part of a scene. However, the available light is variable. A scene shot in bright sunlight is millions of times brighter than a scene lit by a candle. No camera can capture this extreme brightness range in a single shot. So cameras cheat with a trick borrowed from nature. The camera estimates the average brightness — the exposure — of a scene and captures a limited range of light and dark values around the average. (Your eyes adapt to brightness changes in the same way.) When the exposure is correct, the captured measurements match the brightness differences in the scene.

Understanding Exposure Settings

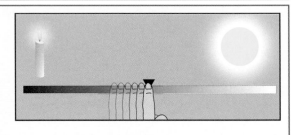

Like all digital cameras, the iPhone and iPad cameras estimate exposure automatically. However, you can use the neat trick described in Chapter 2 to override the camera's guess about the available light to create special effects. More complex cameras always include an automatic exposure option. On some you can also set the exposure manually, often with the help of a built-in light meter. You can use this feature to correct the camera's light estimate — for example, if the light is complex and you want to bring out the detail in one part of a scene.

Understanding Contrast

Contrast is the difference between the brightest and darkest areas in a scene. A shot of a plain gray sky has very little contrast because the brightness is even across the scene. Shots with the light source in front of the camera have a lot of contrast because there is a big brightness difference between the lightest and darkest areas. Cameras do not have a contrast setting because the light in a scene sets the contrast. But you can use iPhoto to modify the contrast in a shot for special effects or to improve the look of a photo.

Understanding Shadows and Highlights

Cameras have to adapt to the average brightness because the range of bright and dark measurements they can capture is limited. The darkest black in a scene is called the black point. The brightest white is called the white point. When the exposure is poor, the black point may be lighter than a pure black, and the white point may be darker than a pure white. The Exposure tool uses a pair of indicators to show you where the black and white points are in your photo. You can slide the indicators to correct obvious exposure errors. On some photos you can push the shadows and highlights to extremes to "pop" the colors.

Understanding Bracketing

Because exposure is always a best guess, your camera sometimes gets it wrong. The easiest way to fix poor exposure is to retake a shot. If your camera has manual exposure control, you can use a professional technique called *bracketing*: Shoot the same scene three or more times starting with an exposure that is slightly too dark, and increasing it until the exposure is slightly too light. This gives you the best chance of capturing a good exposure you can work with. Some cameras have automatic bracketing, and take three or more photos with different exposures in less than a second. The iPhone and iPad cameras lack this feature, but you can often reshoot a scene manually.

Understanding Creative Exposure

You can control exposure creatively to create special effects and change the mood of a photo by controlling light and shadow. Black and white landscapes are often darker than usual to bring out the textures in a scene. Lifestyle photographs and portraits are often shot with a lighter exposure to create a bright and airy feel. You can dramatically improve your photography by looking at the bright and dark balance in professional photos.

Enhance Shadows and Highlights

You can use the Exposure tool to adjust the shadows and highlights in a photo. The tool displays shadows and highlights sliders, and displays the "perfect" shadow and highlight points with a pair of fine lines at the left and right of the control area. It also displays sliders for contrast and brightness, which are described later in this chapter.

To work with the shadows and highlights, drag the two sliders to the left and right. You can ignore the "perfect" positions and experiment with other settings. The results may not be technically ideal, but some photos look better with "incorrect" settings.

Enhance Shadows and Highlights

1 Launch iPhoto and open the editor.

2 Tap a thumbnail to select it for editing.

3 If the Edit button is not selected, tap it to enter edit mode.

4 Tap the **Exposure** icon (⬛).

iPhoto displays controls for shadows, highlights, contrast, and brightness.

5 Drag the shadows slider at the left to adjust the darkest point of the image and set it to black.

Ⓐ The thin line close to the slider shows the "perfect" position.

Ⓑ The area to the left of the slider flashes red if shadows are too dark.

Note: You can ignore the warning if you think the photo still looks good.

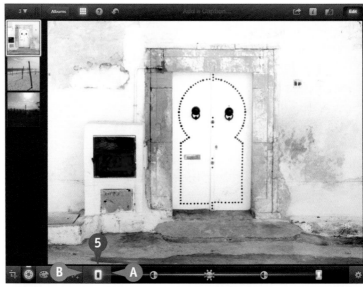

C iPhoto adjusts the shadows to make them darker or lighter.

6 Drag the highlights slider at the right to adjust the brightness of the highlights.

D The fine line to the right indicates the "perfect" highlights exposure.

Note: The area to the right of the line flashes red if you make the highlights too bright, but you may want to do this deliberately.

E iPhoto adjusts the shadows and highlights according to your settings.

Note: The highlights in this photo are deliberately underexposed to reveal the texture of the white wall around the door.

TIPS

Can I change the exposure in a small part of a photo?

The Exposure tool works on complete photos. To adjust parts of a photo, use the Lighten and Darken brushes described in Chapter 9. The brushes give you less control over shadows and highlights, but you can apply them selectively to create more complex effects.

How can I fix a very poor exposure?

All photos capture a narrow brightness range, so there is a limit to the magical power of the Exposure tool. If a photo is badly overexposed, detail in the highlights is lost forever. If a photo is underexposed, you can usually pull detail out of the shadows, but the corrected image will look grainy and the quality will be poor.

Work with Contrast and Brightness

You can use the exposure editor's three central sliders to set contrast and brightness. iPhoto does not display any guides or warnings for these settings, nor does it estimate the "perfect" exposure. So it is up to you to experiment with the settings until your photo looks good.

Contrast and brightness can change the feel of a photo. Less contrast creates a lighter mood. More contrast creates deeper shadows and a darker and heavier mood. Automatic cameras often get the exposure approximately right, so you may not need to do much with these settings.

Work with Contrast and Brightness

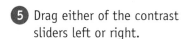

1 Launch iPhoto and open the editor.

2 Select a thumbnail for editing.

3 If the Edit button is not selected, tap it to enter edit mode.

4 Tap the **Exposure** icon (⚙).

5 Drag either of the contrast sliders left or right.

Note: The sliders are linked and move in opposite directions. The closer the sliders, the lower the contrast.

Note: If you move the sliders too close together, some areas in the photo become gray.

Ⓐ iPhoto modifies the contrast, changing the difference between bright and dark areas.

❻ Drag the brightness slider left or right.

Note: iPhoto moves the contrast sliders automatically.

Ⓑ iPhoto adjusts the overall brightness, keeping the contrast unchanged.

Note: The contrast in this photo has been increased to enhance the mood and compensate for the harsh light from the sun. The brightness has been increased to make the foreground stand out.

TIPS

Should I adjust brightness or contrast first?
You can start with either. The settings interact, and you can always undo your changes by tapping the undo icon (■). There is no formula, but you may find it useful to look at your photo with fresh eyes after each edit and think about how you can improve it next.

Can I reset the exposure if I make a mistake?
As with most tools in iPhoto, the settings (gear) icon (✦) displays extra options. You can reset the exposure by tapping the gear icon to show a popover then tapping the **Reset Exposure** menu item. You can also copy and paste the exposure settings to a different photo, although you usually get better results by adjusting the exposure of each photo separately.

Learn about Color

Everyone loves photos with bright colors. iPhoto includes a selection of color editing options that can improve and enhance the color in all your photos. You can also use them to create black-and-white photos from color or to dial down or enhance the intensity of the colors in your shots.

This section introduces the color adjustment tool. You can use it to make colors more or less vivid and to change the color balance in a photo, making it warmer or cooler. The tool also includes special options for working with skin tones. You can use them to improve the look of your portraits, and to adjust colors around your subjects without making them look unnatural.

Understanding Digital Color

Digital cameras capture images by measuring the brightness of a scene on a grid of points called *pixels*. Cameras record color by measuring the amount of red, green, and blue in each pixel. The science of color is complex and cameras sometimes get colors wrong. For example, orange flames sometimes appear purple in photos, and some purple flowers appear blue. But most of the time combining red, green, and blue in different proportions captures most of the colors your eyes can see. If you could look inside a digital photo, you would see a long string of numbers grouped in threes — the red, green, and blue brightness values for each pixel.

Understanding Saturation

Color *saturation* measures how punchy and bright colors are. Black-and-white photos have no saturation at all. A typical photo has medium saturation. Maximum saturation looks garish, blotchy, and unnatural. Many photographers deliberately boost saturation slightly because viewers love bright colors. Landscape photos often have unrealistic saturation, but many photos benefit from a slight boost. Alternatively, you can dial down saturation to create moody or vintage looks. iPhoto's color tools can create both effects.

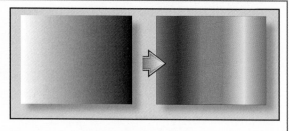

Edit Colors Individually

iPhoto's color saturation tool controls how vivid the colors are in your photo. It includes extra sliders you can use to adjust the individual colors in a photo. But be careful — these sliders do not modify red, green, and blue in a simple way, so they may not create the results you expect. You can use them for independent adjustment of sky and cloud blues, foliage greens, and skin tone reds and pinks. The slider effects are designed to help you and make editing easier. But the results can be difficult to predict, especially if you are used to the more straightforward color editing in other software.

Work with Skin Tones

The skin tone adjustment increases the amount of pink/orange in a photo. It is a subtle effect that gives portraits a warmer and healthier look. You can also use it to add warmth to photos lit by bright blue skies. The effect on darker reds is

less obvious. Usefully, the color adjustment tool includes a Preserve Skin Tones option. You can use it to try to keep skin tones lifelike as you adjust other colors.

Adjust Greenery

The foliage/green slider changes the brightness of mid-green foliage. You can use it to make grass and leaves stand out more in your photo. If you exaggerate the effect it creates an unnatural look because foliage appears to be lit differently from the rest of your photo.

Enhance Sky Blues

This slider creates a complex result. It does not just make blues brighter — it seems to vary the overall contrast and brightness of background lighting. White or gray parts of a scene become brighter even if they are not noticeably blue.

Other colors become more saturated, and overall contrast increases. This slider has a very obvious effect, so take care when using it. Dialing down the blue slider while dialing up skin tones can add a subtle, interesting glow to the complexion of your models.

Add and Remove Color

You can use the Color tool's saturation slider to set the amount of color in your photo. Drag it to the left to make colors less vivid. Drag it to the right to make them more intense. At the far left the slider removes all color, leaving a black-and-white photo.

The slider is sensitive and small movements create big changes. For best results, fix the colors in your photo first using the white balance tool and the other color sliders. Adjust the saturation only after the colors look good.

Add and Remove Color

1 Launch iPhoto and open the editor.

2 Tap a thumbnail to select it for editing.

3 If the Edit button is not selected, tap it to enter edit mode.

4 Tap the **Color** icon (▦).

5 Drag the saturation slider to the far left.

iPhoto removes the color from the photo, leaving a black-and-white image.

6 Drag the saturation slider to the far right.

iPhoto exaggerates the colors and makes the look unnatural.

7 Position the saturation slider slightly to the right of the middle.

iPhoto pops the colors slightly without making them too bright.

Note: This position works well on most photos.

TIPS

Can I make desaturation more dramatic?
Removing color by desaturating a photo can leave it looking bland. You can use the black-and-white effects introduced in Chapter 10 to create more complex results. The black-and-white effects give you more control over how colors are converted to black-and-white. For example, you can make blue skies darker or lighter.

Can I add color to a black-and-white photo?
Some cameras add special effects — for example, you can save black-and-white photos. iPhoto cannot add colors back to a black-and-white photo. You can hand-paint colors onto a black-and-white photo with a more complex editor such as Photoshop Elements for Mac/PC or Photoshop for iPad. iPhoto does not have this feature.

Work with Different Colors

You can use the three color sliders in the color editor to control the amount of skin tone warmth, the brightness of the sky and backgrounds, and the vividness of foliage.

If you are changing the colors in a portrait, you can also use a Preserve Skin Tones option to keep your subjects looking natural. The blue slider has the most vivid effect, so use it first. Experiment with the foliage slider if the photo needs it. Finish by adjusting the warmth slider.

Work with Different Colors

1 Launch iPhoto and open the editor.

2 Select a thumbnail for editing.

3 If the Edit button is not selected, tap it to enter edit mode.

4 Tap the **Color** icon ( ).

5 Move the saturation slider slightly to the right to highlight the changes you are about to make.

6 Drag the blue skies slider slightly left or right to make the sky darker or brighter.

Note: This slider has a big effect. Big movements create distorted results. Try small movements left and right and see which looks better.

7 Drag the greenery slider left and right to make foliage and grass more or less obvious.

Note: Moving the slider all the way to the right can make grass unnaturally bright. Try moving it in both directions to see which result looks best.

Note: This example deliberately makes the grass darker.

8 Drag the warmth slider left and right to add or remove a subtle warm coloring.

Note: This slider has a very subtle effect. It is most obvious on skin tones in portraits. You may find it hard to see the difference on other photos.

Note: This example deliberately makes the photo cooler to emphasize the blue of the sky and the sea.

TIPS

Why do the color sliders work so differently?
Apple has tried to create an editing tool that does what users need. Color adjustments can be complex, and more powerful software has many options. The skies/warmth/foliage approach is effective for simple edits. It is not as flexible as more complex effects, but it is easy to use.

What other color editing options can I use?
The white balance tool described in the next three sections can create more complex color effects. Although it is designed to correct colors, you can use it creatively to change the mood and feel of your photos.

Understanding White Balance

Ideally, you would like all the colors in your photo to be accurate. In practice, lighting conditions vary, so all photos have slightly inaccurate colors. Cameras try to fix this problem automatically, but camera software does not always get it right, even when set up correctly.

You can fix color shifts after you take a photo with iPhoto's white balance tool. You can compensate for specific kinds of light — indoor incandescent, outdoor shade, outdoor sunny, flash, and so on. You can also correct colors manually by pointing iPhoto at a gray or white feature in a photo and leaving it to correct the colors for you.

What Is White Balance?

If you take a photo of white paper you should get a white result. In practice you rarely do. The true color depends on the surrounding lights. Candles and incandescent bulbs have an orange and yellow *cast* — an all-over tint. Blue skies add a cool blue cast. White balance deliberately shifts the colors in your photo to compensate for the way the scene is lit. When you fix

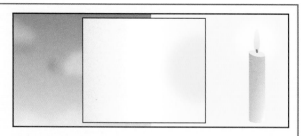

white balance errors, whites in your scene lose their tints and become white again, and all the other colors become more accurate.

Recognize White Balance Errors

When you know what to look for, white balance errors are easy to spot. Indoor scenes often look yellow. Outdoor scenes can be too cold and blue. Scenes taken in shade often have a slight brown and orange cast. If you are not sure if the colors in your photo are correct, look at the whites and grays. If they are tinted, the white balance is wrong and you may need to fix it.

Understanding White Balance Correction

White balance is a complex process and applies two different color corrections. Luckily, you do not need to understand the details to use it successfully. iPhoto's correction tool makes it easy to fix color problems with a few taps. Note that you cannot fix white balance problems with iPhoto's other color tools. White balance changes colors in a unique way, and no other tool produces exactly the same effect.

Understanding Camera White Balance

Cameras, including budget cameras, attempt to manage white balance as you take a photo. Most cameras are set to manage white balance automatically. Some include manual white balance options, so you can choose a setting that matches the lighting conditions to give your camera the best chance of getting an accurate result. Unfortunately, in-camera white balance does not always work as it should. Some cameras are set incorrectly, whereas others do not do a good job of correcting color errors. So even if your camera has this feature you may still need to correct your photos in iPhoto.

Fix White Balance Automatically

iPhoto includes a selection of white balance presets. You can fix white balance by applying a preset that matches the light you used to take the photo — for example, you can select sun, cloud, flash, shade, incandescent lighting, and fluorescent lighting. The presets are fixed, so you have no control over how they correct colors.

Fix White Balance Manually

If you need finer control over white balance, iPhoto includes two manual options. Both display a *loupe* — a graphic of a magnifying glass — which you can move to set a reference point for color correction. One option is designed to use skin tones as a reference, and the other works with any white/gray point in a photo.

Work Creatively with White Balance

Your eyes adjust white balance automatically, so you rarely notice the color differences between indoor, outdoor, and artificial lighting. Viewers looking at snaps are very tolerant of white balance errors. Few viewers care that an indoor snap posted on someone's Facebook wall is slightly yellow. White balance is important for landscape, portrait, or nature photography, where colors should have maximum impact. However, photographers sometimes change the white balance incorrectly to change the mood of a scene, making scenes cooler or warmer with blue or orange. Feel free to keep photos that look good even if the colors are distorted.

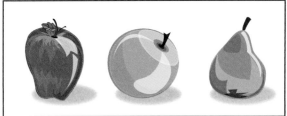

Using a White Balance Preset

You can use one of the white balance presets to apply a standard white balance correction to your photo. For example, if you know your photo was taken under a cloudy sky, you can apply the Cloudy white balance preset.

You can apply a preset by tapping the White Balance icon in the toolbar and tapping one of the further icons in the popover. To see a list of names, tap the help button first. Note that although technically white balance is designed to correct colors, you can also use it creatively to apply an all-over color shift.

Using a White Balance Preset

1 Launch iPhoto and open the editor.

2 Tap a thumbnail to select it for editing.

3 If the Edit button is not selected, tap it to enter edit mode.

4 Tap the **Color** icon (▦).

5 Tap the **White Balance** icon (▧).

Ⓐ iPhoto displays a popover with a list of white balance presets.

6 Tap the help icon (❓) to see the names of the presets.

Ⓑ iPhoto displays the names above the popover.

Note: Many users find it difficult to remember the meaning of each symbol, so remember that you can see their names if you tap the help icon (❓).

7 Tap each preset in turn until you find the one that makes the colors look most natural.

Note: The WB preset matches the white balance estimated by the camera.

Note: In theory, the presets correct for different lighting conditions. In practice, try them all and use the one that works best.

8 Tap anywhere outside the popover to hide it.

iPhoto adjusts the white balance in the photo.

C iPhoto displays the preset icon to remind you which preset you selected.

Note: In this example, the Sun preset brightens the blue in the sky and removes a slight orange cast, making the colors more accurate.

TIPS

Are these presets standard?
There are no official industry standard white balance presets. But many cameras and photo editing tools offer an identical selection. Cheaper cameras may lack a few of the presets, and expensive cameras and software may occasionally include a few more, including some you can specify yourself.

What is color temperature?
If you look up white balance online you may find references to *color temperature*, which is a measure of color in units called Kelvins (K) derived from physics. The theory is complex, but in outline iPhoto uses color temperature values when it fixes white balance errors.

Fix White Balance Manually

You can use two special modes to correct white balance manually. Both display a *loupe* — a virtual magnifying glass. To correct white balance, move the loupe to a point with a reference color. The white balance tool takes that color and corrects it, shifting all the other colors in the photo by the same amount.

The Face Balance loupe is designed to fix skin tones. Move it to a bright area of skin. The Custom loupe is designed to correct whites and grays. Both tools can create dramatic color shifts if you deliberately misplace them. The results often look surreal, but sometimes they can unexpectedly enhance a photo.

Fix White Balance Manually

1 Launch iPhoto and open the editor.

2 Tap a thumbnail to select it for editing.

3 If the Edit button is not selected, tap it to enter edit mode.

4 Tap the **Color** icon (⬤).

5 Tap the **White Balance** icon (⬤) to show the white balance popover.

6 Tap the **Face Balance** preset icon (⬤) in the popover.

A iPhoto plays a sound and displays the loupe.

7 Drag the loupe around the image to find a reference skin tone shade.

B iPhoto estimates the white balance from the point you select.

Note: You may need to move the loupe over most of your subject's face to find a good color.

8 Tap the **White Balance** icon again.

9 Tap the **Custom Balance** preset icon (■).

Note: This example demonstrates how to work with Face Balance and Custom Balance. In practice you apply one or the other — the order does not matter — and keep the one that looks best.

10 Move the loupe until the color is good.

11 Tap the **White Balance** icon again to hide the loupe and lock in the change.

Note: The Custom Balance option creates more extreme color shifts. This example deliberately exaggerates the reds.

TIPS

What is the difference between Face and Custom mode?

Face mode is designed for portraits and creates small shifts, whereas Custom mode creates extreme color shifts. In theory, you should place the loupe on a white or gray area. In practice, you typically move the loupe around the scene until you find colors that look good.

How can I get more accurate colors?

Professional photographers use expensive white/ gray/black or full-color reference cards with ideal colors. Simulate a white reference card with a sheet of paper. Take a shot with the paper close to your subject but off to one side, so you can crop it out later. Place the loupe on the paper in iPhoto, and you should get accurate color correction.

CHAPTER 9

Using Brush Effects

iPhoto's brush effects provide a palette of powerful and subtle tools for fixing, improving, and transforming photos. You can use them to fix small blemishes and problems in photos; to subtly improve photos to add color, contrast, and impact; and to enhance the mood with soft focus and selective color effects. Brush effects are easy to understand, but you may need to practice with them to create the best possible results.

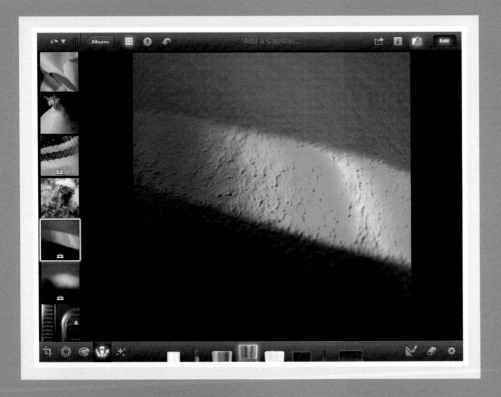

Understanding Brush Effects

You can apply brush effects to parts of a photo by "painting" them with a finger. You can set the intensity of each effect to make it more or less obvious. You can also paint with an eraser to remove the strokes. Many effects support "layered" painting. The effects get stronger and more obvious the more times you brush an area.

The effects appear as a set of animated brushes that fold out from the bottom of the screen. When you begin painting, the brush tips move to the bottom of the screen. Select a different effect by tapping a different brush.

Using Brush Effects

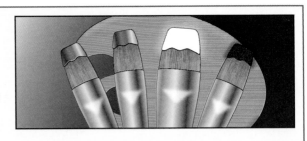

Brush effects are perfect for quick fixes and subtle creative enhancement. iPhoto's other editing tools can fix obvious problems or apply a dramatic transformation. You can use the brush effects to create more subtle improvements. Because you may want to "paint" an entire image, you can also apply a brush effect to all of a photo with a single tap, and set the intensity of the effect with a slider. The brushes can be tricky to work with. When you "paint" with an effect it may take a few goes to create the effect you want, so do not be afraid to experiment and practice.

Understanding the Repair Brush

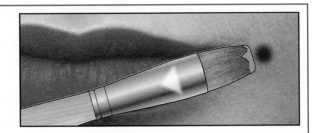

You can use the Repair brush to remove minor skin blemishes. The brush works by copying color and texture and softening detail. To use it, "paint" around the blemish you want to remove but avoid crossing important lines in the image. If you make the painted area too big, the brush creates a waxy and unnatural look.

Work with Color

The Saturate and Desaturate brushes are similar to the Color slider introduced in Chapter 8. You can use the Saturate brush to pop colors and make them stronger, and the Desaturate brush to make colors less intense. You can set the intensity of both effects with a hidden slider, and apply an all-over saturate or desaturate effect. Subtly increasing the saturation improves most photos and is particularly useful for portraits. Too much saturation looks garish and unnatural. You can use the Desaturate brush to create special effects, including selective color — where most of a photo is black-and-white, and only the subject is in color — and vintage or romantic looks with muted colors.

Lighten and Darken a Photo

You can use the lighten and darken brushes to make parts of a photo lighter or darker. As with the Saturate and Desaturate brushes, you can control the intensity with a slider and apply the effect to the entire photo with a couple of taps. You can use both effects to "relight" a photo after you take it, making some areas brighter to emphasize them or darkening other areas to add impact or enhance the mood. These simple effects can create subtle and powerful results.

Undo, Erase, and Control Brush Effects

Hidden options give you more power. You can "paint" with the eraser to remove an effect from parts of a photo. You can use a "detect edges" feature to force an effect to work on areas with matching color and lighting. You can also apply an effect to a photo with a single tap, control the intensity of an effect, remove individual effects, and zoom into a photo to work on small areas with a finer brush. These options are easy to work with - after you know where to find them.

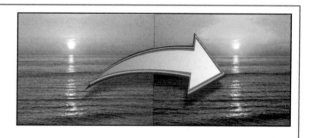

Create Artistic Effects

Because you have almost infinite control over the location and intensity of each brush stroke, you can use brush effects very creatively. Most photos look better with brighter colors and improved contrast, and the brushes are good for these simple improvements. You can also create effects that transform the impact of a photo. You can make a foreground subject stand out from the background, add a dreamy atmosphere, darken the mood, and so on. Chapter 11 has some examples. The possibilities are limited only by your imagination.

Manage Brush Effects

You can get better results if you explore important settings for each effect before you begin brushing. You can access the settings through a popover.

Tap the settings (gear) icon to display the popover. Different brushes have different options. You can erase the strokes for a single effect or for all effects, as described later in this chapter. Some brushes also give you an intensity slider, an option to view strokes, and a one-tap option to apply the effect to the entire image.

Manage Brush Effects

1 Launch iPhoto.

2 Tap a thumbnail to select a photo for editing.

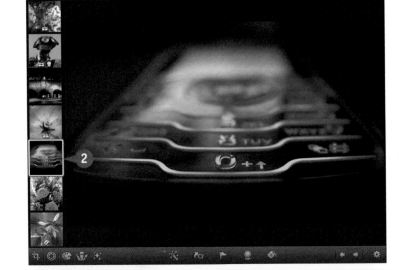

3 Tap the **Brush Effects** icon ( ).

iPhoto displays a selection of brushes and dims the edit area.

4 Tap a brush to select it.

Note: This example uses the Saturate brush.

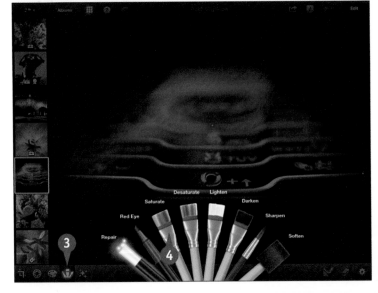

Ⓐ iPhoto moves the brushes to the bottom of the screen, and highlights the brush you selected.

⑤ Tap the settings (gear) icon (⚙) to reveal the settings popover for the brush.

Note: All brushes have different settings.

Note: If you dragged the thumbnail grid to the other side of the screen as described in Chapter 4, the settings (gear) icon appears on the left instead of the right.

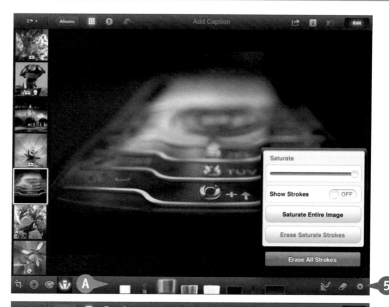

⑥ Drag the strength slider (where available) to change how much each stroke modifies the image.

⑦ Tap **Show Strokes** to see which areas you have stroked with the brush.

⑧ Tap **Entire Image** to automatically apply strokes to the entire photo.

⑨ Tap **Erase Strokes** to remove the strokes for this brush, and **Erase All Strokes** to erase all effects for every brush.

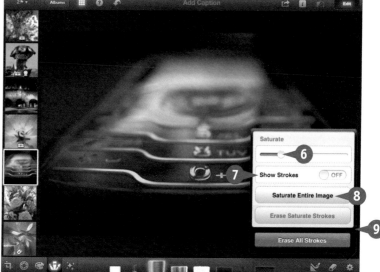

TIPS

What does Show Strokes do?

When you select **Show Strokes** and begin brushing, iPhoto displays your strokes in red. You can instantly see where you have applied an effect. You can use this feature to avoid blotches created by imprecise brushing.

Does the effect strength slider affect each stroke?

The slider sets the strength of all strokes. You cannot apply some strokes with one strength, move the slider, and apply more strokes with a different strength. However, most of the brushes support *layering* — brush an area three or four times, and the effect gets stronger with each stroke.

Zoom for Fine Control

In some editing packages you can set the size of a brush for coarser or finer effects. iPhoto does not have this feature, but you can paint with a "smaller" and more detailed brush by zooming into a photo. You can also pan around the photo to work with different areas.

To zoom, use the standard pinch-zoom gesture. To pan, drag the image with two fingers. (Dragging with one finger applies the brush, so you must use a different gesture for panning.)

Zoom for Fine Control

1 Launch iPhoto.

2 Tap a thumbnail to select a photo for editing.

3 Tap the **Brush Effects** icon ( ).

4 Tap any brush to select it.

Note: This example uses the lighten brush, but you can zoom and pan with any brush.

5 Pinch out to zoom into the photo.

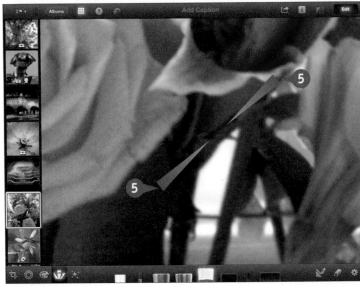

6 Drag with two fingers to move the zoomed area.

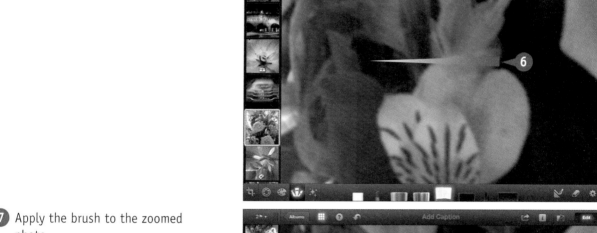

7 Apply the brush to the zoomed photo.

Note: Because the photo is zoomed the effective brush area is smaller, giving you finer control and making it easier to keep the effect within a small area without blotching or smudging.

TIPS

Can I zoom out to simulate the effect of a bigger brush?

iPhoto always fits a photo to the size of the preview area. You cannot zoom out further to make the photo smaller and the brush bigger. So there is no way to paint with very large brushes.

What is the maximum zoom factor?

You can zoom most photos by a factor of 3 to 4. The maximum zoom depends on the size and the resolution of the original photo. This zoom factor gives you enough resolution for fine edits.

Repair a Photo

Photos — and subjects — often have blemishes. You can use the Repair brush to fix minor skin blemishes and improve the look of your photo.

The Repair brush can be tricky to work with. If you apply thick strokes at the standard resolution, the brush creates unattractive waxy blurs. For good results, zoom the photo first and work with the smallest possible strokes. Tap the undo icon to undo individual strokes if you make a mistake.

Repair a Photo

1 Launch iPhoto.

2 Tap a thumbnail to select a photo for editing.

3 Tap the **Brush Effects** icon ( ).

4 Tap the **Repair** brush to select it.

Note: If you have already applied the Crop, Exposure, Color, or Effects tools, iPhoto "peels back" the photo to reveal a fresh view.

5 Pinch-zoom and drag to select the area of the photo you want to improve.

Note: For good results, always zoom in.

6 Carefully apply the brush to part of the portrait.

Note: The red brush stroke fades almost immediately and iPhoto shows the repaired area under it.

Note: Try to use small strokes or dots on areas with similar lighting. Do not stroke across shadows or highlights. Try to follow the natural contours of the face.

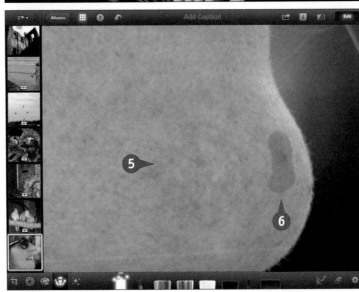

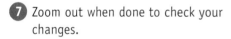 Do not stroke across lines, details, or edges, because the repair brush smudges them.

Note: If you make a mistake, tap the undo icon ().

7 Zoom out when done to check your changes.

Note: This example shows repairs to the, nose, cheeks, and chin.

Note: The finished repair should be realistic without waxy smoothness or blurred details. Keep some imperfections for a more natural look.

Note: This example deliberately over-repairs the nose to show how too much retouching can look unrealistic.

TIPS

What does the repair brush do?
The brush paints detail from the surrounding photo into each stroke. The detail is softened and blurred, making the result smoother. If you paint with very coarse strokes, you can clearly see the blurring effect.

How can I get good results with this brush?
Try to paint along lines and areas with similar lighting, creating a result that keeps the light and shade of the original. Do not brush across details. Human eyes are very sensitive to the structure and lighting of faces. If you change the look too much you can distort the original, making it unnatural and unbelievable.

Remove Red Eye

Red eye is a striking and unwelcome effect that can appear in photos taken with a budget camera. As the name suggests, subjects appear to have sinister red eyes. Cameras produce it when an on-camera flash unit is too close to the lens and reflects light from inside the eye.

You can try to remove red eye with the Red Eye brush, but sometimes it does not work very well. To use it, simply tap each pupil. If your photo has enough resolution, you can also try to remove red eye with the Desaturate brush.

Remove Red Eye

1 Launch iPhoto.

2 Tap a thumbnail with red eye to select it for correction.

3 Tap the **Brush Effects** icon (■).

4 Tap the **Red Eye** brush to select it.

5 Tap the pupil of one eye to apply the brush.

Note: The brush displays a brief expanding circle animation if you tap the pupil correctly. If you miss the pupil it displays a circle and shakes it from side to side.

6 Repeat for the pupil of the other eye.

7 Pinch-zoom to the biggest possible size to check the results.

Note: The brush inserts a dark circle over the pupil, but often misses some areas and removes the highlights from the eyes.

8 If you do not like the result, tap the settings (gear) icon (⚙).

9 Tap **Clear Red Eye Repairs**.

10 Tap the **Desaturate** brush to select it.

11 Very carefully tap and drag slightly over the pupil of one eye.

12 Repeat for the other eye.

Note: If you make a mistake, tap the undo icon (◼).

Note: Often, as in this example, the brush is too big for the pupil. This technique may remove some of the color from the iris and the rest of the eye.

TIPS

How can I get more accurate results?
Sometimes you can get cleaner edges around the pupil if you turn on the Detect Edges feature which is described toward the end of this chapter in the section "Edit Matching Areas." But unfortunately fixing red eye is difficult, and it may not be possible to get a perfect result.

How can I avoid red eye when taking a photo?
Some cameras trigger the flash twice to narrow the pupils of your subjects' eyes and make red eye unlikely. If you have a separate handheld flash, try moving it away from the camera lens. You can also try bouncing light off the ceiling. A few smaller cameras work well if you hold your finger close to the flash when it fires, diffusing the light.

Make Colors Pop

You can use the Saturate brush to make colors pop in your photo. The brush has the same effect as the saturation slider in the color editor, but you can "paint" the effect into a photo for extra control. Many photos look good with some subtle extra saturation, especially portraits and landscapes.

Because you can saturate some areas while leaving others unchanged, you can use this brush to add saturation and avoid the artifacts that can appear if you saturate an entire photo. You can use this effect to highlight some parts of a photo, making the entire image more appealing.

Make Colors Pop

1 Launch iPhoto.

2 Tap a thumbnail to select a photo for editing.

3 Tap the **Brush Effects** icon (⬚).

4 Tap the **Saturate** brush to select it.

5 Brush over an area or feature to highlight it.

Ⓐ iPhoto increases the color intensity, drawing attention to the area.

Note: The effect can be subtle. Tap the settings (gear) icon (⚙) and use the strength slider to make it more or less obvious.

6 Brush further areas to make them more prominent and to highlight other parts of the photo.

7 For a more complex effect, brush along lines or edges to lead viewers to the features you want to emphasize.

Note: This example is slightly exaggerated to demonstrate the effect.

TIPS

When would I paint saturation into a photo?
Faces in portraits often look better with slightly enhanced color, but be careful not to overdo the effect and make your subjects bright orange instead of a healthy warm pink. Generally, you can draw attention to parts of a photo by making the colors stronger. Often this means popping the foreground, but you can try different possibilities to see which works best.

How can I get finer control?
If your fingers are wide you can pinch-zoom to expand the photo for finer control. You can also paint more finely with an optional iPad stylus, available at affordable prices (less than $10) from many online stores. The stylus tip is thinner than a finger and gives you very accurate control.

Remove Color Selectively

You can use the desaturate brush to tone down the colors in parts of a photo. Desaturation is more of a creative effect than saturation. You can use it to highlight a subject by removing some of the color from the background, or to add atmosphere by fading colors deliberately.

This example removes one color from a photo. For a more striking and complex effect, you can use the same tool to remove all colors except those in or around your subject.

Remove Color Selectively

1 Launch iPhoto.

2 Tap a thumbnail to select a photo for editing.

3 Tap the **Brush Effects** icon (▨).

4 Tap the **Desaturate** brush to select it.

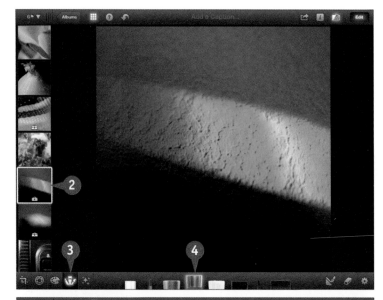

5 Stroke with the brush to remove color from an area.

Note: Optionally, you can tap the settings (gear) icon (⚙) to show the effect settings and use the strength slider to make the effect stronger or weaker.

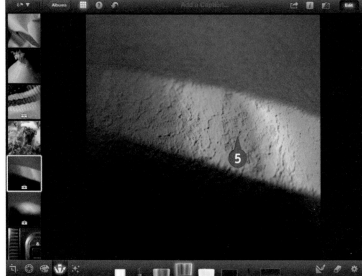

6 Pinch-zoom and drag to apply a smaller brush to important edges in the photo.

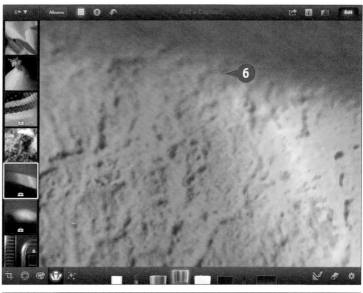

7 Zoom out again to check your work.

Note: This example is a demonstration. For a more typical application use the effect to remove color on or around a model.

Note: As this example shows, unfortunately the effect may not be strong enough to remove all color.

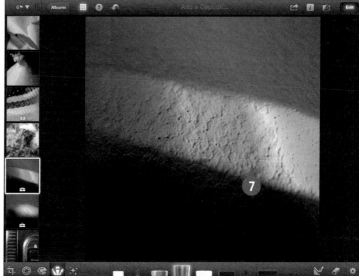

TIPS

Why would I deliberately remove color?
Chapter 11 has some examples of creative editing. Color removal can create some very striking effects, but you can also use it for more natural results. Weaker colors can suggest a gentler mood, especially when combined with effects like vignetting, which is also described in Chapter 11.

How can I select areas more precisely?
The Edit Matching Areas option described later in this chapter works well with the saturation and desaturation tools. It remembers the first color you tap and works on areas with a similar color. For example, if you tap the sky and drag your finger down onto a landscape, the brush stops working outside the blue areas. This makes color selection very easy.

Add Emphasis and Lighten a Photo

Y ou can use the lighten brush to make parts of your photo lighter. Creatively, you can "relight" your photo after you take it to bring out areas in shadow. You can also use the brush correctively to improve the exposure of a photo, but use the exposure editor introduced in Chapter 8 first because it creates a more obvious result.

The lighten effect is too subtle for dramatic corrections, but you can use it to emphasize parts of a photo by making them slightly brighter. This catches the viewer's eye even when the edit is too subtle to be obvious.

Add Emphasis and Lighten a Photo

1 Launch iPhoto.

2 Tap a thumbnail to select a photo for editing.

3 Tap the **Brush Effects** icon ( ).

4 Tap the **Lighten** brush to select it.

5 To create a highlight effect, brush around an area or feature.

6 For more complex effects, zoom and pan to "relight" a feature or area, carefully keeping the effect inside the lines that define it.

Note: This example lightens the area under the overhang.

Note: Because the area is very dark, the result is slightly blotchy. The lighten effect can only lift the brightness of areas that have good detail in the shadows.

7 Zoom out to check your work.

Note: This example brightens the area under the overhang, and also the corner and window to the left, bringing out some of the details lost in shadow in the original.

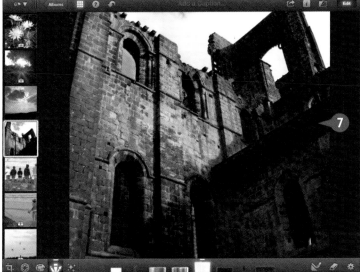

Add Impact and Darken a Photo

You can use the darken brush to darken parts of your photo and place it into virtual shadow. Like the lighten brush, the effect is subtle. But if you apply the brush to a photo and then compare it with an unedited version, you can see that it can make a big difference to the mood of the photo.

You can use the brush to add extra contrast and "bite" to areas as well as darken them. Use it when a photo is slightly overlit and you want to give it more weight, depth, and impact.

Add Impact and Darken a Photo

1 Launch iPhoto.

2 Tap a thumbnail to select a photo for editing.

3 Tap the **Brush Effects** icon (■).

4 Tap the **Darken** brush to select it.

5 Brush an area to darken it.

Note: The flowers and plants in this example are slightly overexposed. Darkening them adds contrast and subtly enhances their impact.

6 Darken a wider area to enhance the effect.

Note: In this example, darkening the wall and the flowers gives weight and impact to the right-hand side of the photo and balances the shadows around the door.

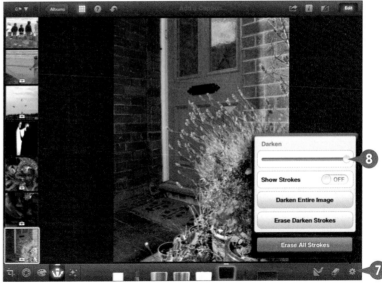

7 Tap the settings (gear) icon (⚙) to display the effect settings.

8 The default slider setting is around 75%. Drag it to the right to make the effect stronger.

Note: The slider resets itself to 75% every time you use this brush.

When would I darken a photo?
Photographers often darken and lighten areas deliberately to enhance the impact of a photo. You can darken the area around a portrait to make the subject stand out more. This effect also works well if you darken an entire photo and use the erase brush to remove the darken effect from the point of interest.

How can I make the effect darker still?
Applying the effect to an entire photo usually makes it dark enough. If you want to create an even darker result, you can save a version of the photo to the camera roll, reload it, and continue brushing. For details see Chapter 11.

Sharpen Parts of a Photo

You can use the sharpen brush to add sharpness selectively. Sharpening a photo is another way to make an area stand out. You can also combine the effect with the soften brush for a more powerful and striking result.

The sharpen brush is subtle and the effect can be difficult to see. For good results use it on areas with plenty of fine detail, such as hair. The effect makes lines and edges stand out, but it needs clean and sharp edges to work with.

Sharpen Parts of a Photo

1 Launch iPhoto.

2 Tap a thumbnail to select a photo for editing.

3 Tap the **Brush Effects** icon (⬚).

4 Tap the **Sharpen** brush to select it.

Note: This example demonstrates the effect on a zoomed photo to emphasize it.

5 Brush an area to sharpen it and highlight the details.

6 Tap the settings (gear) icon (⚙) to show the settings popover.

7 Tap **Sharpen Entire Image** to apply the effect to the entire photo.

8 Tap the strength buttons to select the intensity of the effect.

Note: Unlike the other effects, sharpen can look good applied to a whole photo, but it can also enhance noise and grain.

iPhoto sharpens the entire image, highlighting all the details.

Note: Sharpening the entire image always creates a more intense effect than applying the sharpen brush.

TIPS

Why does this effect do nothing?
To highlight the effect, tap the original/edited button and compare your changes with the original photo. You should see that the painted areas are clearer and sharper. If not, try a different photo with cleaner edges. At extreme settings you may see a subtle bright halo around objects, especially against a plain background.

Can I correct a blurred photo?
You cannot fix a badly blurred photo. The sharpen effect needs edges to work with, and a badly blurred photo does not have them. The blur is "burned into" the photo, and no tool or effect can remove it. However, you can improve the impact of a slightly soft photo by giving it more bite and clarity.

Create Soft Dreamy Effects

You can use the soften brush to deliberately blur your photo. You can often improve a portrait by blurring the area around it. Features such as hair and clothes can also look good if you soften them.

This brush supports layering. Areas become softer as you brush them over and over. You can typically brush four or five times before the effect reaches a maximum. You can use this feature to create soft-focus areas, or to improve the skin on a portrait without making it look waxy and unrealistic.

Create Soft Dreamy Effects

1 Launch iPhoto.

2 Tap a thumbnail to select a photo for editing.

3 Tap the **Brush Effects** icon ( ).

4 Tap the **Soften** brush to select it.

5 Brushing around the edges of a photo often creates a good look.

6 For a more extreme effect, brush everywhere except for the areas you want to highlight.

Note: This example brushes around and between the roses, making them stand out.

7 Tap the settings (gear) icon (⚙) to show the settings popover.

8 Tap the strength buttons to vary the intensity of the effect.

Note: The Soften Entire Image option does not look good, even at the weakest setting.

TIPS

Why is the Soften Entire Image effect so strong?
Softening the entire image is like applying multiple strokes to all of it. This option works well on some of the brushes, but the softening effect is too strong to be useful on most photos — it simply blurs the entire image.

Is this effect similar to soft focus?
Photographers create soft-focus effects by shooting through layers of crinkled plastic wrap or smearing transparent gel on glass in front of the lens. The soften brush can create similar results, but you must apply it selectively to create a convincing result.

Edit Matching Areas

The Edit Matching Areas option works like an assistant that remembers the color and texture of the area you first tap. If you drag your finger onto some other color, the assistant disables the current brush.

You can use this feature to trap an effect inside an area. If your fingers are wide, it can be difficult to avoid painting over boundaries, creating smeared results. The Matching Areas option helps keep your edits clean and precise.

Edit Matching Areas

1 Launch iPhoto.

2 Tap a thumbnail to select a photo for editing.

3 Tap the **Brush Effects** icon (image).

4 Tap any brush to select it.

Note: This example uses the Saturate brush, but the effect works with any brush you select.

5 Tap the **Detect Edges** icon (image).

A iPhoto highlights the icon.

6 Tap on or inside an area with a distinct color.

7 Without lifting your finger, brush around the area.

8 Repeat for similar areas in the photo.

B iPhoto "traps" the brush effect inside an area with a color that matches your tap.

Note: Colored areas often have bright edges and the effect does not detect them accurately, so the "trapped" area may be slightly too small.

9 Repeat for other areas you want to edit.

Note: You can tap any other brushes to select them and they will all "trap" an effect in the same way.

TIPS

When would I use this feature?
The best way to explore this feature is to experiment with it. It can be quirky and unpredictable, and it can also work very well indeed. Try it whenever you want to apply any brush effect to a limited area. It may or may not do what you need. When it does, it can save you a lot of time.

Why is it not working?
This option works well on areas with clean and distinct colors and sharp edges. More complex textures and edges with distinct colors can confuse it. For more accurate control over edges, zoom into your photo and paint around the difficult edges by hand. You can then zoom out and apply a wider brush to the areas in between.

Erase Brush Effects

The brush effects give the best results with practice, persistence, and skill. Fortunately, you can undo and redo changes until you create the result you want by tapping the undo icon. You can also remove all the strokes for a single effect or for all effects, as described in the section "Manage Brush Effects."

But you may also want to correct brush strokes by hand. You can use the Undo brush to remove some or all of a brush effect. It cancels the effect of an existing stroke. You can "paint" it on your photo until you create the result you want.

Erase Brush Effects

1. Launch iPhoto.

2. Tap a thumbnail to select a photo for editing.

3. Tap the **Brush Effects** icon (⬢).

4. Tap the **Soften** brush to select it.

5. Tap the settings (gear) icon (⚙) to show the effect settings popover.

6. Tap **Desaturate Entire Image**.

A iPhoto removes the colors from the image.

7 Tap the **Undo** brush icon ().

8 Brush an area to remove the effect.

Note: In this example, brushing restores color to a selected part of the sky.

9 Brush a different area "by accident."

10 Tap the undo icon ().

iPhoto undoes the effect of the Undo brush and restores the original effect.

Note: Use this option if you make a mistake with the Undo brush ().

TIPS

Is the Undo brush a corrective or creative tool?
You can use it either way — there are many applications. One option is to zoom into a photo and make very small corrections around lines and edges. But you can also use it creatively, as demonstrated in this section.

Does the Undo brush have an intensity setting?
No, nor does it support layering. If you brush over an existing effect, it completely removes that effect. You cannot use it to tone down an effect or to make it less intense.

CHAPTER 10

Using Filters and Effects

You can use iPhoto's effects to transform your photos in dramatic ways. Instead of subtly enhancing a photo, you can totally transform its look and mood to create visually striking effects that were once only available to professionals. The effects are easy to use, but because they can be unpredictable the best way to master them is to experiment. This chapter introduces the simpler effects. Chapter 11 explores further creative experiments.

Understanding Effects

You can modify your photos in creative ways by applying various effects. Most create dramatic results — for example, you can change a color photo into a black-and-white one, or convert a photo into a painting. The Warm & Cool effect can create more subtle adjustments.

The effects appear on animated fold-out strips. You can select an effect by tapping a strip, and then modify the effect by dragging your finger left and right. You can also modify some effects by dragging your fingers on the photo.

Understanding Photo Effects

In the days of darkroom editing, photographers evolved a range of extreme special effects. iPhoto includes digital versions of many of these popular wet-paper, lens filter, and darkroom effects. The enhancements and corrections introduced in Chapter 8 add subtle improvements to a photo. The effects in this chapter are much more dramatic. You can use them to completely transform the look and the mood of a photo and to create images that look creative, unusual, and "photographic."

For best results, choose your source photo carefully, but do not be afraid to experiment. If you do not like an effect, you can always restore the original photo. Note that iPhoto can only apply one effect at a time, but you can save an edited photo to the camera roll, re-open it, and apply another effect.

Understanding Color Effects

Chapter 8 discussed how to enhance the color of a photo. The color filter effects can do much more. For example, the Black & White effect removes all the color from a photo, and it also allows you to choose how colors map to brightness. You can make a blue sky a dramatic shade of dark gray, or a much brighter white. The Aura effect is even more complex. It converts most of a photo into black-and-white, but leaves one or two selected colors.

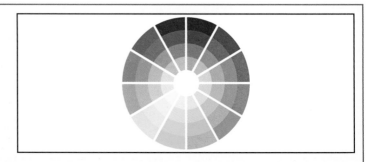

Understanding Duotones

Duotones are one particular color effect. Visually, a duotone looks like a black-and-white photo overlaid with a subtle tint. A true chemical paper duotone uses a complex process that adds a hint of color and enhances the midtones — middle-brightness grays — to increase the impact of the photo. iPhoto uses a simpler process

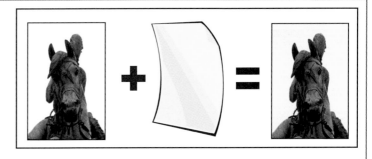

to create an approximation of the real effect. For even better results you can enhance the photo further by changing the exposure as described in Chapter 8. You can also restore some of the original colors to create an unusual blended result with austere but dramatic colors.

Understanding Vignettes and Highlights

An optional vignette effect is built into three filters — Black & White, Vintage, and Artistic. You can use this feature to darken the corners or edges of a photo, adding romantic distance to your photo and highlighting one area. This is not a complicated effect, but it can dramatically

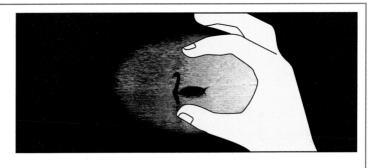

enhance the mood of a photo. You can set the width of the vignette by pinching with two fingers and move the center by dragging with one.

Understanding Artistic Effects

iPhoto includes a selection of popular art-look effects in the Artistic filter. Landscape photographers often create dramatic skies by using a plastic or glass filter over the lens with a *gradient* effect — a thick deep color, often orange or gray, that shades to transparency toward the middle of the frame. iPhoto includes three

gradient effects with subtly different color tints. You can also blur the top and bottom of a photo to create an effect called *tilt-shift*, which creates photos that look like miniature scenes. You can add *ink effects* to create attractive painted photo edges. And you can experiment with two paint-like filters that mimic brush strokes on canvas or paper. This chapter introduces the paint-like effects. The other artistic effects are introduced in Chapter 11.

191

Add Ink Effects

You can make your photos look more artistic by adding an *ink effect* to the edges of the photo. Unlike a photo, hand-drawn art is never a perfect rectangle because the edges are often smeared or textured.

You can create a similar result with the ink effects in iPhoto, applying one of six ready-made borders. The effect includes a color saturation slider so you can fade or pop the colors to heighten the mood. The ink effects are simple but they can look great on cards and small prints.

Add Ink Effects

1 Open the thumbnail browser.

2 Tap any thumbnail to select a photo for enhancement.

3 If the bottom toolbar is not visible, tap the **Edit** button.

4 Tap the **Effects** icon (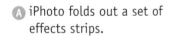).

Ⓐ iPhoto folds out a set of effects strips.

Note: The original photo is darkened when the strips appear.

Note: The strips include tiny preview thumbnails of each effect at different settings.

5 Tap the **Ink Effects** strip to select the ink effects.

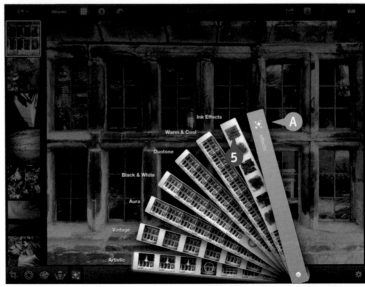

B iPhoto moves the Ink Effects strip to the bottom of the screen, ready for editing.

6 Tap one of the preview thumbnails on the strip to select an effect.

C iPhoto adds a hand-drawn or hand-painted border to the photo.

Note: Tap the thumbnails to apply the different borders.

7 Slide your finger on the saturation bar to tone down or boost the colors in the photo.

TIPS

Can I customize the ink effects?
The border shapes and textures are fixed and you cannot import borders or create your own. But if you drag one finger up and down you can set the intensity or "bite" of the effect. You can also drag a finger left and right to change the color saturation.

Why do the colors change when I boost them?
The saturation slider applies a complex color shift that tries to mimic the look and feel of a pastel drawing. Blues are popped more than other colors. The effect is not the same as the color boost introduced in Chapter 8.

Create Warm and Cool Colorings

The Warm & Cool effect is designed to change the color balance of a photo. You can shift the balance slightly toward red for warmth, or toward blue for coolness. The effect is useful for adding life to portraits and for wintry or watery landscapes.

On other photos, you may find it difficult to see a difference. The results are very subtle and depend on the colors in the source photo and the quality of your iPad's display. You can see the effect more easily on the improved retina display on the 3rd and 4th generation iPads and on high-quality paper prints.

Create Warm and Cool Colorings

1 Open the thumbnail browser.

2 Tap any thumbnail to select a photo for enhancement.

3 If the bottom toolbar is not visible, tap the **Edit** button.

4 Tap the **Effects** icon (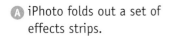).

A iPhoto folds out a set of effects strips.

Note: The original photo is darkened when the strips appear.

5 Tap the **Warm & Cool** strip to select the Warm & Cool effect.

(B) iPhoto moves the Warm & Cool strip to the bottom of the screen, ready for editing.

(6) Tap the strip.

(C) iPhoto displays a light blue indicator line.

(7) Slide your finger on the indicator to the left to add more red and warm up the photo.

(8) Slide your finger to the right to add more blue and cool down the photo.

Note: The effect is subtle.

TIPS

Why does this filter do nothing?
The effect can be very subtle. Look closely at the colors and move the sliders between the extremes to see a difference. You should be able to see it working on any portrait photo taken in bright sunlight. The cooler extreme can enhance seascapes and snow scenes.

How do I remove an effect?
Tap the undo icon (⬛) in the top toolbar. You can also tap the settings (gear) icon (⬛) in the lower toolbar and tap **Remove Effect**. You can find the settings (gear) icon on the bottom corner of the screen, on the opposite side from the thumbnail grid.

Master Duotones

You can use the Duotone effect to create black-and-white images with a hint of color. Simple black-and-white can look austere and lackluster. A subtle tint creates extra impact.

You can set the tint color, but not the tint intensity. Be careful to avoid a muddy result. Blue, orange, and purple tints often look good. Yellow is less useful. You can also add back muted versions of the original colors. The results are unpredictable — some photos look good, others become garish and weird.

Master Duotones

1 Open the thumbnail browser.

2 Tap any thumbnail to select a photo for enhancement.

3 If the bottom toolbar is not visible, tap the **Edit** button.

4 Tap the **Effects** icon (■).

5 Tap the **Duotone** effect strip.

Ⓐ iPhoto moves the Duotone strip to the bottom toolbar, ready for editing.

Note: You can preview the effect by viewing the thumbnails in the strip.

6 Tap anywhere on the strip to create a duotone.

 iPhoto displays a light blue indicator marker on the strip.

7 Slide the marker left and right to select the tint color.

8 Tap the **Color** icon ( ) to add back some of the original color.

Note: You can toggle the Color icon by tapping it again.

What can I do with duotones?
Duotones are "black-and-white but better." Viewers often do not notice the hint of color, but the duotone effect is more eye-catching than a plain black-and-white photo. The creative applications are almost endless. Simple images with a clean composition work best because duotones highlight shapes and textures.

Is this filter a good way to create a sepia look?
Moving the slider to the fifth or sixth thumbnail from the left creates a subtle sepia effect. The Black & White tool described in the next section includes a less subtle sepia option.

Convert Color to Black-and-White

You can use the Black & White effect to remove the colors from your photo. The color adjustment tool introduced in Chapter 8 also removes colors. The Black & White effect is more sophisticated, and includes many extra features.

You can control how colors map to different shades of gray, to lighten or darken skies and grass. You can also add film *grain* — subtle specks that add texture to a photo. The filter also includes a single-tap sepia option, which overlays a tan color for a vintage look. And finally, you can add a vignette effect.

Convert Color to Black-and-White

1 Open the thumbnail browser.

2 Tap any thumbnail to select a photo for enhancement.

3 If the bottom toolbar is not visible, tap the **Edit** button.

4 Tap the **Effects** icon (▓).

5 Tap the **Black & White** effect strip.

A iPhoto moves the Black & White strip to the bottom of the toolbar.

6 Tap the toolbar to convert the photo to black-and-white.

B iPhoto displays a light blue indicator marker on the strip.

7 Slide your finger left and right to change how colors are mapped to shades of gray.

Note: Small movements can make a big difference.

⑧ Tap the **Vignette** icon (◯) to darken the corners of the photo.

Note: You can find out more about the vignette effect in the next chapter.

⑨ Tap the **Grain** icon (◉) to add film grain to the photo.

Note: Film grain is subtle and may only be obvious if you close the editor and zoom into the photo.

⑩ Tap the **Sepia** icon (◉) to create a vintage look with a light tan overlay.

Note: You can tap the icons again to turn off the effects.

TIPS

How can I understand color mapping?
If you find — or take — a photo of a rainbow or a color spectrum, you can use it as a reference to see how the filter converts color to brightness. But you do not need to know the details to create a good result. The best approach is to experiment with the slider position until you find a setting that works for you.

When would I add film grain?
Without color, black-and-white images rely on texture. The small speckles added by the film grain effect add an all-over texture that makes a photo appear more eye-catching with extra depth and character. Without it, digital photos taken in bright light can look smooth and plastic. Photos taken in poor light usually have grain of their own and do not need more.

Pick Out Strong Colors

You can use the Aura effect to copy a striking photographic technique that is often used in creative photography and advertising.

The Aura effect creates a black-and-white photo with selected color highlights. The results are unpredictable and depend on the colors in the original scene. You cannot select the colors with any accuracy, but you can use the effect to create quirky and interesting hybrid photos, such as a black-and-white landscape under a blue sky.

Pick Out Strong Colors

1. Open the thumbnail browser.

2. Tap any thumbnail to select a photo for enhancement.

3. If the bottom toolbar is not visible, tap the **Edit** button.

4. Tap the **Effects** icon (🔲).

5. Tap the **Aura** effect strip.

Ⓐ iPhoto moves the Aura strip to the bottom of the toolbar.

6 Tap the strip at the far left to remove all the colors.

B iPhoto displays a light blue indicator bar and removes the colors from the photo.

7 Slide your finger to the right to restore a range of colors.

C iPhoto converts part of the photo to black-and-white but keeps selected colors.

TIPS

How can I get more control over color selection?
The Aura filter cannot match the powerful color selection tools available in a professional photo editor. But you can use the Desaturate brush introduced in Chapter 9 to "paint" a similar effect with your fingers.

Which photos work best with the effect?
For portraits, make your subject wear a single strong color that clashes with the background. For other subjects, use photos with strong areas of red/orange, green, or blue. Although the effect is difficult to fine-tune, it can often pick out single colors for you.

Create Vintage Film Effects

You can use the Vintage effect to re-create popular vintage film looks. Vintage photos often have muted or incorrect colors because the colors have faded. Some films deliberately over-emphasized reds and oranges for better-looking skin tones.

You can select one of six standard effects — Early Chrome, Sixties, Saturated Film, Neutral Film, Vivacious, and Muted. The best way to understand them is to try them all with different source photos. The color and contrast of your starting image make a big difference to the result.

Create Vintage Film Effects

1. Open the thumbnail browser.

2. Tap any thumbnail to select a photo for enhancement.

3. If the bottom toolbar is not visible, tap the **Edit** button.

4. Tap the **Effects** icon (⬛).

5. Tap the **Vintage** effect strip.

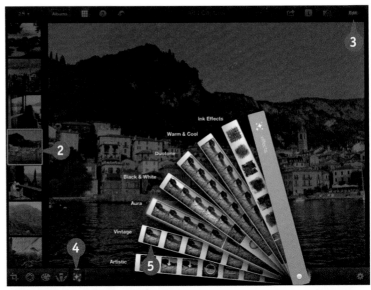

Ⓐ iPhoto moves the Vintage strip to the bottom of the toolbar.

6. Tap the help icon (❓) to view the name of each effect.

7 Tap one of the thumbnails to preview an effect, such as the Early Chrome thumbnail.

8 Tap the **Vignette** icon (○) to remove the vignette effect.

Note: The Vintage effect always adds a vignette effect. You must turn it off if you do not want it.

iPhoto applies the effect.

9 Tap the other effect thumbnails to explore what they do, such as the Sixties thumbnail.

Note: The thumbnails apply different effects. You cannot use a slider to move smoothly between them.

TIPS

Can I modify the vintage effects?
No, the effects are preset and you cannot change them. However, you can re-create most of the effects manually using exposure and color adjustments. For example, to copy the Early Chrome effect, push in the highlight and shadow sliders of the Exposure tool to decrease the contrast, and use the Color tool to turn down the saturation.

Can I modify the vignette effect?
You can adjust the vignette in the usual ways. Pinch with two fingers to shrink or expand the darkened area. Drag the center of the vignette to change its position.

Convert a Photo into Art

You can use the Artistic filters to turn photos into paintings. People find art interesting because it hints at shapes, colors, and scenes, and distorts images in interesting ways. The paint-effect filters in iPhoto simulate two of the many possible ways a photo can be turned into art.

The filters have no settings, so you cannot change what they do. For good results, modify the color and exposure of a photo before applying a filter. Art often distorts color and contrast. You can create a more realistic painted effect by starting with a photo you have modified in unrealistic ways.

Convert a Photo into Art

1 Open the thumbnail browser.

2 Tap any thumbnail to select a photo for enhancement.

3 If the bottom toolbar is not visible, tap the **Edit** button.

4 Tap the **Effects** icon (■).

5 Tap the **Artistic** effect strip.

Ⓐ iPhoto moves the Artistic strip to the bottom of the toolbar.

6 Tap the help icon (❓) to view the name of each effect.

7 Tap the **Oil Paint** thumbnail to view the oil paint effect.

iPhoto applies the oil paint effect.

Note: The effect softens hard edges and removes detail, but does not simulate brush strokes.

8 Tap the **Watercolor** thumbnail.

iPhoto applies the watercolor effect.

Note: The effect breaks up the image into lightly textured areas of color.

Can I make these effects look more like paintings?
iPhoto's paint-like effects are very simple. You may not find them very convincing if you have worked with real watercolors, oils, and acrylics. Unfortunately these effects have no settings. You can use them as they are, or not at all. But do try modifying the color and exposure of a photo before you apply them.

What do the other Artistic filters do?
The other Artistic filters are photographic and do not attempt to simulate a painted look. You can use them to add colored gradients, blur the top and bottom of the image, or add a vignette. For details, see the next chapter.

CHAPTER 11

Creating Advanced Photo Effects

You can combine iPhoto's effects for impressive creative results. This chapter introduces recipes for a few advanced effects and explains how you can take iPhoto further by creating your own.

Understanding Advanced Editing

Once you master the basic features of iPhoto, you can begin to explore more advanced effects. Some advanced effects are built-in one-tap effects. For example, you can use the tilt-shift effect in the Artistic effect strip to transform your photos into miniature scenes. Other effects are more open-ended, and you may need to combine multiple steps to create the result you want.

One-Tap Advanced Edits

The Artistic effect strip in iPhoto includes powerful ways to enhance photos with a single tap. The *gradient* effects apply a smooth color shading from the top of the photo. You can use them to enhance the sky in landscapes and outdoor photos, and to add atmosphere to some interior shots. The quirky *tilt-shift* effect blurs

the top and bottom of a scene, creating an unusual optical illusion that makes outdoor scenes look like miniatures. You can set the size and position of the blurred area to maximize the illusion.

Enhance Mood and Impact

iPhoto has many options, and it can be difficult to master them without a guide. Concentrating on mood and impact helps you make more sense of iPhoto's features. You will find editing becomes less technical and more emotional and creative. The best photos have a definite mood and a strong visual impact — often a blend of

clean shapes, a clear subject, and strong colors or textures. If you try to bring out these features as you work, you may be surprised how easy it is to convert snaps into eye-catching images.

Ask Creative Questions

Because you can transform your photos in so many ways, it is good to have a guide. For inspiration, take any photo from a website, book, or magazine, and pull it apart to see how it works. Look at the colors, the shapes and composition, and the emotional impact of the subject or scene. Look especially at how the

photo distorts reality. Are the colors realistic, muted, or exaggerated? Are they shifted towards red, green, or blue? Are parts of the photo deliberately blurred or darkened to lead your eye to the subject? Are there strong lines or other shapes? Once you understand the look, you can experiment with the tools in iPhoto and try to re-create it.

Experiment

You can never destroy a photo by editing it, so you can experiment without worrying that you may lose your favorite images. Mistakes are essential for creativity. With iPhoto you can experiment with your photos as much as you want. Once you know how to save versions, you can keep experimenting over and over, starting with the same photo or with different variations.

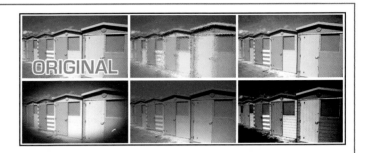

Understanding the iPhoto Workflow

iPhoto is designed with a *workflow* in mind — a standard sequence of edits that can help you create a good result. Typically you crop and rotate a photo, correct or modify its exposure, correct the color, and perhaps apply a brush effect. You can apply one of the artistic effects, but you can apply only one effect at a time. iPhoto uses a page flip

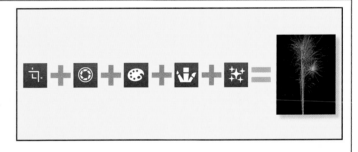

display to show partially modified versions of a photo as you work on it. This can be confusing; the secret is to understand that iPhoto shows the result of one tool at a time. The flipped view shows the combined result. It is visible only when you finish working with each tool, effect, or brush set.

Combing Effects

You can break out of the standard workflow with a simple trick that gives you extra creative choices. Simply save a photo to the camera roll after each major edit, and reload it for further work. You can use this trick to apply any combination of tools, effects, or brushes in any order. You can also apply the same effect more than once — for example,

you can apply two vignette effects with different centers. Best of all, you can produce multiple versions of the same photo and keep the ones you like best.

Add a Color Gradient

Professional photographers sometimes use a gradient filter (*grad*) — a piece of glass with a fading color tint fitted in front of a camera lens. The bottom half of the glass is transparent. Photographers use grad filters to darken skies, make clouds more obvious, and add drama to landscapes.

You can simulate the effect of a grad filter with iPhoto's Color Gradient effect, which adds a warm orange, cool blue, or neutral gray tint. You can change the width and position of the gradient and rotate it through 360 degrees for creative effects.

Add a Color Gradient

① Open the thumbnail browser.

② Tap any thumbnail to select a photo for editing.

③ If the bottom toolbar is not visible, tap the **Edit** button.

④ Tap the **Effects** icon (▓).

⑤ Tap the **Artistic** effect strip.

Ⓐ iPhoto moves the strip to the bottom toolbar, ready for editing.

⑥ Tap the first thumbnail to add a gray gradient.

⑦ Pinch with two fingers to set the upper and lower edge of the gradient.

8 Tap the second thumbnail to add a warm gradient.

Note: iPhoto cancels the previous gray gradient and adds a warm gradient.

Note: On its own this gradient may look gray, but if you compare it with the previous gray effect, you can see it is a sepia color.

9 Pinch with two fingers to set the gradient.

Note: You can rotate the gradient by twisting your fingers.

10 Tap the third thumbnail to add a cool blue gradient.

11 Pinch and rotate the gradient to position it.

Why are there three color options?
You can match the gradient to the strongest colors in the scene and to change the mood of a photo. The blue gradient works well on sunny midday photos with blue skies. The red effect is good for scenes taken around sunrise or sunset with warm colors. The gray effect can work on almost any photo, but it lacks the punch of the colored gradients.

Is it better to use a real glass filter?
You may not have a choice, because not many budget cameras support glass filters, although more expensive SLR cameras usually do. A good glass filter usually produces more dramatic and striking results than a software effect but the effect becomes part of the photo. In iPhoto you can add the effect later and adjust it until it looks good.

Work with Vignettes

You can use the vignette effect to simulate a vintage look, hide clutter, and to draw the eye to one part of a scene. Vignettes are simple but powerful. Viewers do not usually notice a subtle vignette effect consciously, but they do notice that the photo has a different mood.

The vignette effect is built into the Black & White and Vintage filters, and is also a stand-alone filter on the Artistic effect strip. All versions are identical and work the same way. You can pinch to change the size of the vignette, and drag its center point with your finger.

Work with Vignettes

1. Open the thumbnail browser.

2. Tap any thumbnail to select a photo for editing.

3. If the bottom toolbar is not visible, tap the **Edit** button.

4. Tap the **Effects** icon (▦).

5. Tap the **Artistic** effect strip.

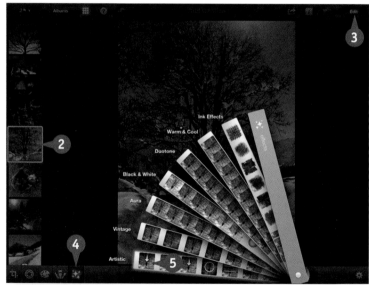

A. iPhoto moves the strip to the bottom toolbar, ready for editing.

6. Tap the fourth thumbnail to create a vignette.

B iPhoto adds the vignette and darkens the corners of the photo.

7 Pinch the photo with two fingers to change the size of the vignette.

8 Drag your finger on the photo to change the center of the vignette.

Note: Be careful to keep the effect subtle. Too much can make a photo feel claustrophobic. Sometimes you may want to do this deliberately.

TIPS

When would I use a vignette?
Experiment with a vignette when you want to add atmosphere to a photo. A good tip is to track your eyes when you look at the photo. Where do they spend the most time? Adding a vignette can control a viewer's point of interest. You can enhance the effect by using the Soften brush to blur the darkened area.

Can I change the shape of the vignette?
The vignette is always a circle. You can change the size of the circle so it covers only the edges of the image, and you can move the center of the circle. iPhoto does not support square or rectangular vignettes.

Create a Fake Miniature

You can use the tilt-shift effect to blur a photo deliberately and make it look like a miniature model. The effect simulates a narrow *depth of field* — the size of a photo's in-focus area — creating the illusion of a tiny scene shot from close-up. You can also use the effect with portraits to blur the foreground and background, assuming the model is near the center of the shot.

For a good result, start with a photo of a distant scene. Buildings surrounded by tiny cars and people work best.

Create a Fake Miniature

1 Open the thumbnail browser.

2 Tap any thumbnail to select a photo for editing.

3 If the bottom toolbar is not visible, tap the **Edit** button.

4 Tap the **Effects** icon (▦).

5 Tap the **Artistic** effect strip.

Ⓐ iPhoto moves the Artistic strip to the bottom toolbar, ready for editing.

6 Tap the fifth thumbnail to create the tilt-shift effect.

Ⓑ iPhoto blurs the top and bottom of the image.

7 Pinch the photo with two fingers to change the size of the blurred area.

C iPhoto displays two lines to mark the edges of the blurred area.

8 Drag your finger on the photo to move the blurred area up and down.

Note: The closer you move the two lines, the stronger the effect.

Note: You can rotate the lines with your fingers, but the effect is usually stronger if you keep them horizontal.

iPhoto makes the photo look like a miniature.

TIPS

When would I use the tilt-shift effect?
This is a striking effect and a handful of professional photographers have built their careers around it. But because it is so quirky and unusual, you are unlikely to use it often. However, you can also use this effect to add top/bottom blur on portraits. The results are less specialized and can be more useful.

Why is it called tilt-shift?
The effect can be created optically with a special camera/lens combination. The lens can be tilted to shift the focus point in the scene. The iPhoto effect looks almost as good but is very much cheaper to buy.

Add Mood and Atmosphere

You can use any of iPhoto's editing tools to add mood and atmosphere to a photo. Each photo is different, but you can usually make an obvious improvement by adjusting color saturation and exposure. You can also use the soften brush to add soft focus effects.

This example creates a very obvious enhancement — sometimes dramatic changes can look good. The next two examples in this chapter demonstrate how to create more subtle improvements.

Add Mood and Atmosphere

1 Open the thumbnail browser.

2 Tap any thumbnail to select a photo for editing.

3 If the bottom toolbar is not visible, tap the **Edit** button.

4 Tap the **Exposure** icon (⬛).

5 Move the black-point slider to darken the shadows.

6 Move the white-point slider to brighten the highlights.

7 If the photo needs it, use the central sliders to enhance the contrast.

8 Tap the **Color Editor** icon (⬛).

9 Drag the saturation slider to the right to bring up the colors.

10 Drag the skin tone slider to the right to warm up the photo and make it redder.

11 If the photo needs it, drag the green and blue sliders to the right for even more color.

Note: Not every photo needs every step. Aim to increase the power and impact of the photo.

Note: The colors in this example are deliberately exaggerated for effect.

⑫ Tap the **Brush Effects** icon (⬛).

⑬ Select the **Soften** brush.

⑭ Stroke your finger on the photo to soften the subject and the background.

Note: This example softens the girl's hair and the foreground detail to bring out the dreamy and artistic mood of the original photo.

Note: You may need to undo and repeat the coloring and softening until you get a result you like.

TIP

Is there a summary of tools and effects?

The variations are almost endless, and the best way to explore them is to experiment. Here are some tips to get you started.

Tool/Effect	Result/Application
Soften brush	Create areas of dreamy soft focus
Lighten brush	Brighten a subject — similar to fill-in flash
Darken brush	Darken a background
Increase color saturation	Add richness and warmth
Decrease color saturation	Create coolness, starkness, and distance
Lighter exposure	Create a lighter, more delicate mood
Darker exposure	Add drama and weight
Vignette	Create a more distant, reflective mood

Improve a Portrait

You can use the tools and effects in iPhoto to enhance portraits and make them more appealing and eye-catching. Improving a portrait has no set recipe, so use the basics of photography — color, light, emotion, and composition — as a guide. Look at a photo before you try to improve it. How well does each element work, and how can you make it work better?

This example uses a photo of a baby with good composition and strong emotion. The lighting and color can be improved with editing.

Improve a Portrait

1 Open the thumbnail browser.

2 Tap any thumbnail to select a photo for editing.

3 If the bottom toolbar is not visible, tap the **Edit** button.

4 Look carefully at the photo to find ways it could be improved.

5 Look especially at the lighting and color of the main subject.

Note: In this example the face is slightly dark, the colors are not very strong, and there is limited contrast between the subject and the background.

6 Select the **Brush Effects** icon ( ).

7 Tap the **Saturate** brush to improve the color.

8 Carefully paint the face to bring out the natural warmth.

9 Paint the hands and to make them more colorful.

Note: The saturation in the example is slightly exaggerated for clarity.

10 Select the **Lighten** brush.

11 Paint the face to lighten the brow and remove the shadow.

Note: The lightness in the example is slightly exaggerated for clarity.

12 Tap the **Desaturate** brush.

13 Paint the background around the subject to remove some of the color.

Note: The contrast between the saturated subject and desaturated background brings the subject forward and adds to the impact.

TIPS

Is it always useful to look at background and foreground contrast?

You can improve a portrait in many ways, but creating contrast between the subject and the background is a popular option. You can create contrast with any feature of the photo — exposure, saturation, sharpness, and so on.

Does it matter if the enhancement is obvious?

Aim for enhancements that improve the photo and do not distract the viewer. If you change the original too much, you can create a photo that looks unnatural and obviously fake. But "too much" depends on the audience. Some viewers are happy with obvious edits as long as they like the mood you create.

Prepare a Photo for Framing

You can use cropping and portrait enhancement to improve a photo before you frame it. iPhoto's Crop tool can cut out clutter and resize the photo to match a standard print size. Use the other editing tools to make a portrait more flattering, usually by making the image warmer, smoother, and more colorful.

You can use the effects introduced in the previous chapter to create dramatic portraits — for example, you can use the Aura filter or create a duotone. This example uses more basic edits to crop and enhance a color photo of a model.

Prepare a Photo for Framing

1 Open the thumbnail browser.

2 Tap any thumbnail to select a photo for editing.

3 If the bottom toolbar is not visible, tap the **Edit** button.

4 Look at the photo to see how it can be improved.

Note: In this example the empty space around the subject is unnecessary, and the overall color balance is slightly blue and cool.

5 Tap the **Crop** tool (🔲).

6 Tap the settings (gear) icon (⚙).

7 Select a standard print size.

Note: This example selects the 4 × 3 size.

8 Drag and pinch the photo inside the frame to fill the area with the subject.

9 Use the rotation dial to rotate the subject.

Note: Steps **8** and **9** are to taste; aim for a result that looks good to you.

10 Tap the **Color Editor** icon (⬛).

11 Adjust the sliders to the right to enhance the color.

Note: The settings in this example warm the skin tone and increase overall saturation.

12 Tap the **White Balance** icon (⬛) and select the **Face Balance** preset icon (⬛).

13 Place the loupe on the rock to create a warm red color shift.

14 Tap the **Brush Effects** icon (⬛).

15 Select the **Sharpen** brush.

16 Carefully paint the subject and the water drops to make them stand out.

17 Select the **Lighten** brush and paint the subject to bring the details out of the shadow.

Note: Some portraits work better with softening instead of sharpening.

Note: This example exaggerates the edits for clarity. Changes are usually more subtle.

TIPS

Can I overuse soft focus?
Blur and soft focus are very strong techniques, and they can become distracting if you overuse them. If your subject looks plastic or waxy you have overdone the effect. The best edits are so subtle that most viewers cannot see them without a side-by-side comparison with the original photo.

Why does the photo look different when I print it?
Professional photographers use *color calibration*, a technical process that matches colors in cameras, monitors, and printers. The iPad does not support this, so the colors you see on its screen may not match the colors you see on a different screen or on a paper print. You can compensate by trial and error. If colors are exaggerated on paper, use the color tool to decrease saturation slightly.

Combine Effects

iPhoto does not give you an easy way to apply multiple effects to a photo. The undo feature can step back through edits, but does not save versions for you.

You can fix both problems by saving photos to the camera roll as you edit them. iPhoto treats each saved version as a separate photo. You can edit it from scratch to create unique combined effects. You can delete unwanted versions in the Photos app, or manually when you sync. And you can use this option to load edited photos back into iPhoto on a Mac.

Combine Effects

Note: This is an advanced technique. You do not have to use it, but it is useful to know you can.

1 Open the thumbnail browser, and select any photo for editing.

2 Edit the photo using any of iPhoto's tools and effects.

3 Tap the **Share** icon (⬆).

4 Tap the **Camera Roll** icon.

5 Tap the **Selected** option.

Note: Optionally, you can select and save more than one edited photo at a time using the features introduced in Chapter 4.

6 Tap the **Camera Roll** button.

iPhoto saves the photo to the camera roll, automatically opens the Camera Roll album, and reloads the photo.

7 Use any of iPhoto's editing options to continue editing the photo.

Note: You can repeat steps **3** to **7** every time you want to save a new version to the camera roll.

Note: The most recently saved photo always appears at the top of the thumbnails.

TIPS

Why would I keep different versions?
Because you can dump working versions back to a Mac or PC where memory and storage space are cheap, you can experiment with creating many different interpretations of a photo. A good tip is to save versions as you work, leave them for a day or two, and then look at them with fresh eyes. You will see immediately that some versions work better than others. You can then decide which versions you want to keep.

How can I work on an older version?
Select it from the camera roll. As long as you do not delete the versions from the camera roll, you can select any saved version for further editing. You can use this option to save different versions so you can compare them later, and perhaps start editing from a different point.

CHAPTER 12

Sharing Photos

You can use iPhoto's sharing features to share your edited and original photos with friends and family. iPhoto includes direct support for Twitter, Facebook, and the popular Flickr online album. You can also print and e-mail photos, and save them to the device camera roll or a special iTunes-compatible folder. This chapter explores each option in detail. Chapter 13 explains how to save and share photos in journals.

Learn about Photo Sharing

Photos are more fun when shared. iPhoto includes a full selection of sharing features. You can use them to share photos to social networks, e-mail photos to friends or colleagues, add photos to an online album, print photos, and view them on the iPad or an external display.

You can also copy photos to your Mac or Windows computer and import them into other photo-editing applications. Because the iOS file system is locked down for security reasons, you may need to spend some extra time getting comfortable with these more serious sharing options.

Select and Share

You can access the sharing options by tapping the **Share** icon () which appears near the top right of the main toolbar in the thumbnail browser. The options appear in a popover. You can add photos to a journal; save photos to the camera roll; share photos with iTunes; e-mail, beam, or print photos; share photos to a social network; or create a slide show. You can share more than one photo at a time by selecting or flagging multiple photos. For details see Chapter 4 or Chapter 6. You can also share every photo in the current album or event.

Using Social Networks

Social networks are immensely popular, and you can share photos to both Twitter and Facebook from iPhoto. After you log in — you only need to do this once — you can share photos quickly and easily, adding an optional comment or caption. You can also upload photos to the Flickr photo sharing service, an easy and free way to keep your photo collection safe online and share your favorites with friends and family.

Print and View

With Apple's AirPrint technology, you can send your photos to a Wi-Fi-enabled printer for instant printing. Many budget printers can create small prints with a standard glossy finish, which can rival, or sometimes beat, the colors produced by a commercial photo print service. AirPrint is useful and convenient but not essential. You can also

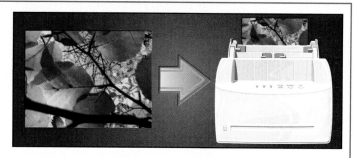

save your photos to a folder that appears in iTunes and print them from a Mac or PC. More expensive printers can create small posters or art prints on larger paper for framing and selling. For less permanent sharing you can also connect your device to a projector or a home TV, with optional horizontal mirroring so they display correctly.

Create Slide Shows

You can create a complex slide show with a few finger taps. Slide shows combine your selection of photos with preset animations and an optional musical backing. You cannot save or share slide shows, but you can view them on a device or on an external display, such as a TV or projector. Although slide shows are limited — you cannot change the

animations or use your own music — they are a simple, fun, and effective way to view photos with friends and family members.

Beam and Save to iTunes

You can beam photos between devices as long as the devices are on the same Wi-Fi network and both are running iPhoto. *Beaming* a photo literally copies it from one device to another. It is a good option for sharing a small number of photos but is not a speedy choice, and is not ideal for sharing large collections. You can also share photos

to a Mac or PC through iTunes. When you next sync your device in iTunes, the photos appear in special folders on the File Sharing page. You can copy the folders to your Mac or Windows hard drives with simple drag and drop.

Save Photos to the Camera Roll

Getting photos into iPhoto is relatively easy. Copying photos out of iPhoto is less obvious, especially when they appear in one of iPhoto's smart albums.

In fact, you can export any photo from any album, event, or photo collection. The trick is to save your photo to the device camera roll. You can then import the contents of the camera roll into iPhoto on a Mac, or copy the photos directly from your device in Windows. To save a photo, access the Share dialog and select the Camera Roll option.

Save Photos to the Camera Roll

1 Open the thumbnail browser for any album or event or for the Photos collection.

2 Tap any thumbnail to select it for saving.

3 Tap the **Share** icon (⬀).

Note: You do not need to be in Edit mode to save a photo.

4 Tap the **Camera Roll** icon.

iPhoto displays the Selection popover.

5 Tap the **Selected** option to save the current photo.

Ⓐ You can tap the **Choose Photos** option to select and save a different photo.

Note: You can only select and save a single photo at a time.

Note: If exactly one photo is flagged, the Flagged option is not grayed out, and you can share that one photo.

B iPhoto displays a progress
bar as it saves the selected
photo to the camera roll.

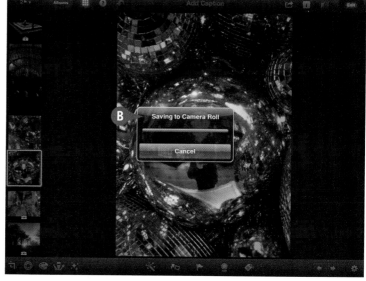

6 Tap **Done** when finished or
Camera Roll to open the
Camera Roll album and view
the photo.

TIPS

How can I share an entire album?
You can only share a single photo at a time
to the camera roll. To share an entire album,
share to iTunes and copy the photos from
iTunes to a folder on your Mac or PC as
described in the next section.

Why does saving to the camera roll create duplicates?
Imported, beamed, or uploaded photos already exist on
your device. Saving them to the camera roll creates
another copy. This is not usually a problem. You can clear
the camera roll by importing the photos to your Mac or
copying them to a Windows PC and deleting the files from
your device. When you clear the camera roll, the
duplicates disappear.

Share Photos with iTunes

You can copy photos from your device to your Mac or PC via iTunes. To use this feature, tap the **iTunes** option in the sharing popover.

iPhoto saves your selected photos to a named folder. To access the folder, connect your device to your Mac or PC, launch iTunes, select your device in the device list, and click the **Apps** option. Scroll down and click **iPhoto** in the File Sharing list to see the folders created by the Share to iTunes option. You can drag the folders from iTunes and drop them on any location in Finder or Windows Explorer.

Share Photos with iTunes

1. Open the thumbnail browser for any album or event or for the Photos collection.

2. Select one or more photos for sharing.

3. Tap the **Share** icon (⬆️).

Note: You do not need to be in Edit mode to share a photo.

4. Tap the **iTunes** icon.

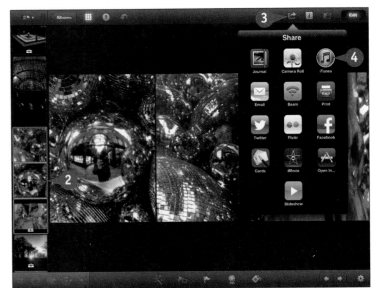

5. Tap the **Selected** option to save the currently selected photos.

Ⓐ You can tap the **Flagged** option to save all flagged photos in the current album or event or in the complete photo collection.

Ⓑ You can tap the **All** option to save all photos in the current album or event or in the complete photo collection.

Ⓒ You can tap the **Choose Photos** option to select one or more other photos.

D iPhoto displays a progress bar as it saves the selected photos to iPhoto's documents folder.

6 Connect your device to your Mac and launch iTunes if it does not launch automatically.

7 Select your device in the Devices list.

8 Click **Apps**.

9 Scroll down to the File Sharing section and click **iPhoto**.

E iTunes displays a list of folders saved from iPhoto.

Note: You can drag folders from the iPhoto Documents list to any folder on your hard drive, and then open them to view or copy the photos inside them.

TIPS

Why are the import and export options on different pages?

The iTunes design separates these features. You can upload photos to your device using the Photos option introduced in Chapter 5. It would be simpler if you could import photos on the same page, but iOS has a secure file system and you can only access some of the files in your device on the Apps File Sharing page.

Why can I not open the folders on this page?

Currently there is no way to open a folder on the File Sharing page in iTunes. To open a folder, first copy it to your Mac or PC. Note that you can delete files and folders on this page by clicking to highlight them, and then pressing `Delete`. (You can also import files by dragging them from Finder or Windows Explorer, but iPhoto ignores them.)

E-Mail Photos

You can share photos by e-mailing them. The e-mail option is a good choice for private sharing. However, you can share only a maximum of five photos in a single e-mail.

The e-mail feature has some hidden options. If you have more than one e-mail account set up on your device, you can tap the sender field to select a different sender. You can also set the image size to send a thumbnail instead of a full-sized image.

E-Mail Photos

1 Open the thumbnail browser for any album or event or for the Photos collection.

2 Select one or more photos for sharing.

3 Tap the **Share** icon ( ).

Note: You do not need to be in Edit mode to e-mail a photo.

4 Tap the **Email** icon.

5 Tap the **Selected** option to e-mail the currently selected photos.

A You can tap the **Flagged** option to e-mail all flagged photos in the current album or event or in the complete photo collection.

B You can tap the **All** option to e-mail all photos in the current album or event or in the complete photo collection.

C You can tap the **Choose Photos** option to e-mail one or more other photos.

Note: Some options are grayed out automatically so you cannot e-mail more than five photos.

iPhoto displays an e-mail composer.

6 Tap the **To:** field to set the recipient.

7 Tap the **Subject:** field to change the subject.

D You can tap **Cancel** followed by **Delete Draft** to cancel.

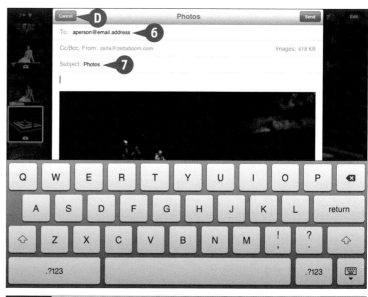

8 Tap the **Cc:** field to show further options.

9 Tap a button to select an image size for the photos.

Note: Select **Small** or **Medium** if sending to someone's phone or tablet.

10 Tap ⊕ to add further recipients.

11 Tap the **Bcc:** field to add further hidden recipients.

Note: Addresses in the Bcc: field are hidden from all recipients.

12 Tap **Send** to send the e-mail.

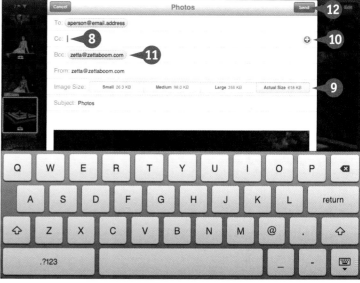

TIPS

Why is e-mail sharing limited?

Many e-mail systems reject large messages. There is no standard maximum size, but 5MB is a practical limit. Messages larger than 10MB are very likely to be rejected. iPhoto deliberately limits the size to avoid this, but keep in mind that if you import photos from a good SLR, a single image can easily be 5MB or more, and you should e-mail a smaller version.

How can I e-mail more images?

The e-mail sharing option is designed for casual sharing among friends and for low-volume business use. iPhoto cannot e-mail tens or hundreds of photos. For professional photo sharing, import the photos to a Mac or PC and use a high-volume service such as FTP (File Transfer Protocol) to upload them to a company web server.

Beam Photos to Another Device

You can *beam* photos to another device. Beaming copies photos over Wi-Fi. The other device must be connected to the same Wi-Fi network, and it must be running iPhoto. You can beam a maximum of 100 photos.

To beam photos, select them and tap the **Beam** sharing option. iPhoto looks for devices on the network that are also running iPhoto for iOS. (As of version 1.1, you cannot beam photos to iPhoto on a Mac.) When you select a device, iPhoto sends a request. If the user accepts the request, iPhoto copies the photos and puts them in a special Beamed album.

Beam Photos to Another Device

① Open the thumbnail browser for any album or event or for the Photos collection.

② Select one or more photos for sharing.

③ Tap the **Share** icon (▣).

Note: You do not need to be in Edit mode to beam a photo.

④ Tap the **Beam** icon.

Note: You must enable beaming in the iPhoto preferences. See Chapter 1 for details.

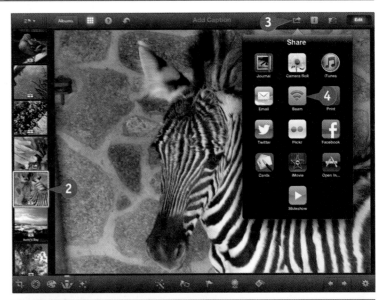

⑤ Tap the **Selected** option to beam the currently selected photos.

Ⓐ You can tap the **Flagged** option to beam all flagged photos in the current album or event or in the complete photo collection.

Ⓑ You can tap the **All** option to beam all photos in the current album or event or in the complete photo collection.

Ⓒ You can tap the **Choose Photos** option to beam one or more other photos.

Note: Options are grayed out if they offer more than a hundred photos.

6 Launch iPhoto on the other device, if it is not running already.

7 Tap the name of the other device in the popover to select it.

8 Tap **Beam Photos** to begin beaming.

iPhoto displays an alert showing that beaming has started.

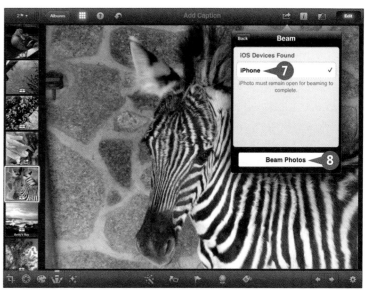

9 On the other device, tap **Yes** when the Accept Photos dialog appears.

10 Wait until beaming completes.

Note: In the current version of iPhoto, the progress bar does not indicate progress while beaming, but beaming is still happening while you wait.

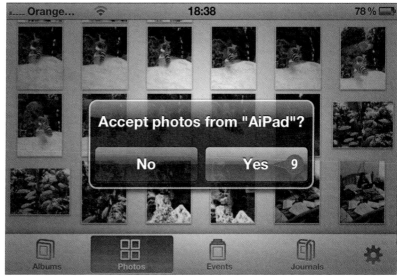

TIPS

How can I save the photos in the Beamed album?
The Beamed album is invisible to iTunes, so you cannot sync the photos in it to your Mac or PC. But you can save photos from the album to the device camera roll, and then import or copy the camera roll from your device to a Mac or PC.

Why is beaming so slow?
Beaming was speeded up in version 1.1 of iPhoto. But the speed still depends on the speed and quality of your Wi-Fi connection. Public Wi-Fi is often slow. Beaming works best with a handful of photos; it can take hours to beam a hundred photos.

Print Photos

You can send photos from iPhoto to any compatible AirPrint printer. The printing option has no settings and works over Wi-Fi. After you select a printer, it "just works." You can select an unlimited number of photos for printing, but you should print only in small batches of ten or so.

Note that you cannot send photos to a commercial print lab from iPhoto. If you have too many photos to print at home, you can upload the photos to Flickr, iPhoto on a Mac, Photoshop Elements on a PC, and similar packages and use the commercial printing features built into those products. Many photo print services also support direct uploading from your photo library via a web page.

Print Photos

1 Open the thumbnail browser for any album or event or for the Photos collection.

2 Select one or more photos for printing.

3 Tap the **Share** icon (▣).

Note: You do not need to be in Edit mode to print photos.

4 Tap the **Print** icon.

5 Tap the **Selected** option to print the currently selected photos.

Ⓐ You can tap the **Flagged** option to print all flagged photos in the current album or event or in the complete photo collection.

Ⓑ You can tap the **All** option to print all photos in the current album or event or in the complete photo collection.

Ⓒ You can tap the **Choose Photos** option to print one or more other photos.

Note: You can select unlimited photos for printing.

6 Tap the **Printer** option to
select a printer.

D You can tap ✚ or ➖ for
more or fewer copies.

7 Tap a printer to select it.

Note: By default, only AirPrint
printers appear in this list. To print
to a standard printer, see the tip.

8 Tap the **Printer Options** button
to return to the previous dialog.

9 Tap the **Print** button to begin
printing.

TIP

Do I have to use a special printer?

In theory you must buy a compatible printer to use AirPrint. For a list of models, see the Apple support
document at http://support.apple.com/kb/ht4356. In practice you can print to any printer attached to a
Mac or PC as long as it is on the same Wi-Fi network. The details depend on your computer and other
hardware. Some printer manufacturers have created their own special drivers — search the web for the
manufacturer's name and "AirPrint." For a general solution for a Mac, search the web for "AirPrint
Hacktivator." For Windows, search for "sc.exe Bonjour AirPrint."

Share Photos via Twitter

You can use the Twitter share option to send a photo with optional text to the popular Twitter service. iPhoto uses your usual Twitter identity and sign-in details. You can share only one photo in each tweet.

Photos appear as Photobucket links in your Twitter feed. iPhoto automatically shrinks the photo to a reasonable size, uploads it to Photobucket, and creates a clickable link. If you add text, it appears above the photo link in your feed.

Share Photos via Twitter

1 Open the thumbnail browser for any album or event or for the Photos collection.

2 Select a photo for tweeting.

3 Tap the **Share** icon (⬆).

Note: You do not need to be in Edit mode to tweet a photo.

4 Tap the **Twitter** icon.

5 Tap the **Selected** option to tweet the current photo.

A You can tap the **Choose Photo** option to select and tweet a different photo.

Note: You can only tweet a single photo at a time.

Note: If exactly one photo is flagged, the Flagged option is not grayed out, and you can tweet that one photo.

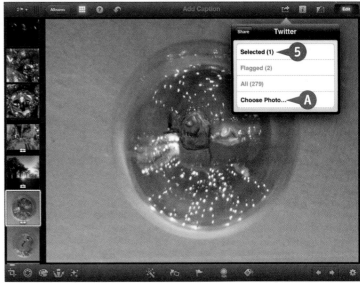

6 Type some text to describe your tweet.

B iPhoto displays the remaining character count as you type.

Note: Tweets are limited to 140 characters.

7 Tap **Send** to send the tweet.

Note: You must have Wi-Fi or mobile data access to send a tweet.

C You can tap **Cancel** to cancel it.

D You can tap the **Add Location** option at the bottom left to include your location with the tweet.

E iPhoto posts the tweet. You and your followers can view it with any Twitter client.

TIPS

Why does iPhoto ask me to sign in?
The Twitter feature uses your device's standard Twitter account. If you have not already signed in, iPhoto opens the Settings app on the correct page so you can enter your details. You only need to do this once. After you sign in, iPhoto always skips straight to the Twitter send popover.

Can I share photos to more than one account?
In iOS, your device can log in to only one account at a time. Currently iPhoto uses the first account you set up in Settings, even if you change the selected account in the Twitter app. So you can send photos only from that one account. There is no way to switch accounts or to send photos from multiple accounts.

Upload Photos to Flickr

You can use the Flickr photo sharing service to share your photos. You can create public and private photo collections and upload tens or even hundreds of photos at a time. However, sharing is slow, so expect to wait a few hours if you attempt to upload an entire album.

Flickr is easy to use. It is managed by Yahoo! and you will need a Yahoo!, Facebook, or Twitter account to use it. iPhoto asks you to sign up or log in before you can share photos, but you only need to do this once on each device.

Upload Photos to Flickr

1 Open the thumbnail browser for any album or event or for the Photos collection.

2 Select one or more photos for uploading.

3 Tap the **Share** icon (📤).

Note: You do not need to be in Edit mode to upload photos.

4 Tap the **Flickr** icon.

5 Tap the **Selected** option to upload the currently selected photos.

Ⓐ You can tap the **Flagged** option to upload flagged photos in the current album or event or in the complete photo collection.

Ⓑ You can tap the **All** option to upload all photos in the current album or event or in the complete photo collection.

Ⓒ You can tap the **Choose Photos** option to select one or more other photos.

Note: You can select unlimited photos for upload.

D You can tap to select a set.

E You can tap to select **Privacy**.

Note: You can select **Private**, **Family**, **Friends**, and **Public** privacy settings to limit access to your photos.

F You can tap **Add Tags** to show a Tag text box.

Note: Tags are optional single-word descriptions that can help you sort and find photos.

6 Tap **Share to Flickr** to upload the photos.

iPhoto displays a progress bar as it uploads the photos, followed by a Done dialog when uploading is complete.

G The photo or photos appear on the Flickr website.

Note: The privacy settings control access to the photos. You can nominate friends and family groups to keep some photos private. For details, see the online help on Flickr.

TIPS

Why would I use Flickr?
Flickr is a popular and widely known photo sharing service. Visitors can view and comment on your public photos. You can also create private collections for friends and family. You can use Flickr as an online album. Some users find it easier to use than iCloud journals. You can also order paper prints and photo books using the Snapfish service.

Do I have to use Yahoo! to use Flickr?
You can log in to Flickr with a Facebook or Twitter account. You do not have to create a separate Yahoo! ID if you do not want one.

Post Photos to Facebook

You can upload one or more photos to Facebook with the Facebook sharing option. By default, the photos are posted to your Facebook Wall Photos album. You can also choose to upload them to one of your other albums.

You must sign in to Facebook before you can post photos, and also give iPhoto permission to send and receive data from your Facebook account. You only need to do this once. After you sign in and set up the account, you can post photos with a few taps. Uploaded photos do not include a description, but you can add one on Facebook.

Post Photos to Facebook

① Open the thumbnail browser for any album or event or for the Photos collection.

② Select one or more photos for posting.

③ Tap the **Share** icon (⬆).

Note: You do not need to be in Edit mode to post photos.

④ Tap the **Facebook** icon.

⑤ Tap the **Selected** option to post the currently selected photos.

Ⓐ You can tap the **Flagged** option to post all flagged photos in the current album or event or in the complete photo collection.

Ⓑ You can tap the **All** option to post all photos in the current album or event or in the complete photo collection.

Ⓒ You can tap the **Choose Photos** option to post one or more other photos.

Note: You can post an unlimited number of photos.

D By default photos are posted to your Wall Photos album, but you can tap the **Album** option to select a different album.

6 Tap **Share to Facebook** to upload the photos.

Note: Sharing can take a long time, especially if you post tens or hundreds of photos.

iPhoto displays a progress bar as it uploads the photos, followed by a Done dialog when uploading is complete.

E The photo or photos appear on Facebook.

F You can click this option to add a description.

TIPS

Are uploaded photos full-sized?
Between them, iPhoto and Facebook shrink photos to a manageable size, usually a few hundred pixels on a side. iPhoto does not upload the original full-sized versions of your photos. Although web users can still download and link to your photos, they cannot make high-resolution prints or copies.

Do the photos include location information?
iPhoto uploads location information to Facebook, and you can add a location to the photo on Facebook if you choose to. However, location information is stripped out of the photo. If someone downloads a photo, he cannot see your location.

Create and View a Slide Show

You can create a live slide show to display your photos with interesting animations and music. Slide shows are a good way to make your photo collections more entertaining. You can select the photos you want to share, or share every photo in an album.

iPhoto creates slide shows "live" as you view them. You cannot save a slide show as a file, copy it to another device, or upload it to iCloud or to a web server. However, you can view a slide show on an external display.

Create and View a Slide Show

1. Open the thumbnail browser for any album or event or for the Photos collection.

2. Select one or more photos for the slide show.

3. Tap the **Share** icon (▣).

Note: You do not need to be in Edit mode to create a slide show.

4. Tap the **Slideshow** icon.

5. Tap the **Selected** option to include all selected photos.

Ⓐ You can tap the **Flagged** option to include all flagged photos in the current album or event or in the complete photo collection.

Ⓑ You can tap the **All** option to include all photos in the current album or event or in the complete photo collection.

Ⓒ You can tap the **Choose Photos** option to select other photos.

Note: You can include an unlimited number of photos, but you must include more than one.

6 Tap to select an animation style.

Note: To see what the animation styles do, experiment with them.

7 Tap this switch to add music.

8 Select the backing track.

9 Tap **Start Slideshow** to play the slide show.

iPhoto plays an animated slide show with optional backing music.

Note: You can tap the screen to show a transport bar with stop, pause, previous, and next buttons.

Note: This example is playing a slide show with all photos selected, not just the photos selected in the previous steps.

TIPS

How can I improve the sound quality?
If you use the built-in speaker on your device, the music may sound thin and tinny. You can connect your device to an external music system with better speakers through a standard 3.5mm adapter lead. Most mall electronic supplies stores stock suitable adapters, but they may be expensive. eBay is a good source for cheap adapters.

Why does iPhoto crash if I select a lot of photos?
iPhoto creates the slide show and saves it before it plays. If your device has too little free memory, iPhoto can crash if it tries to work with too many photos, usually when you try to change the slide show type or select different music. To fix this, create a slide show with a single item, change the animation and music, go back, and reselect all the photos you want to see.

Using Other Sharing Options

You can use other sharing options to do more with your photos. You can view photos on an external display by plugging your iDevice into a projector with a special adapter. If you have an Apple TV, you can use AirPlay to view photos on your television.

You can also share your photos with other apps. In version 1.1 of iPhoto you can copy photos to Apple's Cards and iMovie apps and to selected third-party apps. Unfortunately the app sharing feature is not compatible with popular photo-editing apps. iMovie can accept multiple photos and videos. The other options can share a single photo at a time.

Using Other Sharing Options

Copy a Photo to Cards

1 Select a photo and tap the **Share** icon ( ).

2 Tap the **Cards** icon and tap the **Selected** option.

A iPhoto opens the Cards app, copies the photo to it and pastes it into the standard card templates.

Note: You can only share one photo at a time.

Note: The Cards app is free. Cards cost $2.99 each if mailed within the US and $4.99 if mailed elsewhere.

Copy a Photo to iMovie

1 Select a photo or video and tap the Share icon ( ).

2 Tap the **iMovie** icon and tap the **Selected** option.

B iPhoto opens iMovie app and copies the photo or movie to it so that you can add it to a video or slide show.

Note: You must install iMovie ($4.99) to use this option.

Copy a Photo to Other Apps

1. Select a photo or video.

2. Tap the **Share** icon ().

3. Tap the **Open in** icon and tap the **Selected** option.

4. Tap one of the apps in the popover.

Note: Only a few apps are compatible with photo sharing. Most photo-editing apps are not. There is no guarantee that apps listed in the popover can receive or display photos correctly.

Show Photos on an External Display

1. Connect your iPad via a special adapter to a projector or external monitor.

   iPhoto displays photos on the external display.

Note: You can enable mirroring to display iPhoto as you edit. For details see the section "Investigate iPhoto Settings" in Chapter 1.

TIPS

Which adapter do I need?

Projectors and monitors support four standards — composite video, HDMI, VGA, and DVI. Your display's manual lists the connectors your display works with. The Apple Store sells Apple-brand adapters for the first three types. You can find HDMI to DVI adapter cables on Amazon and eBay.

Can I buy a cheaper adapter?

eBay is a popular source of cheap cables and adapters. However, performance is not guaranteed. The products are usually much cheaper than their official Apple equivalents, but they may not work correctly, so you buy from eBay at your own risk.

CHAPTER 13

Creating Journals

You can use journals to collect and display your photos in attractive documents. Albums and events are simple photo collections. Journals can be decorated with text, notes, quotes, maps, calendars, and even weather reports and recipes. Journals also support full-screen photo viewing, and you can easily share them with friends and family.

Learn about Journals

Journals are a unique feature in iPhoto for iOS. You can use them to present your photos in attractive and creative ways. You can choose the photos you want to include. You can also add further content including quotes, text, maps, weather reports, and recipes.

Journals are more open-ended than iPhoto's albums and events. They make an ideal replacement for paper photo albums. You can arrange photos as you want, highlight some photos by size, and add captions. You can also share your journals to iCloud, and then send friends and family a link to a single journal or your journal collection.

Create a Journal

To create a journal, use the Share popover introduced in Chapter 12 and share one or more photos to a new journal. There is no separate "create a journal" option. You can name a journal when you create it. Note that the name on the Journals page is fixed — you cannot change it later. You can also set the background image and layout style of the journal. iPhoto gives you the option to open the journal immediately after you create it so you can customize the layout and add further content.

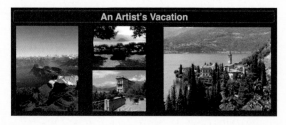

Add Photos and Other Items

You can add as many photos as you want at any time to a journal by selecting an existing journal in the Share popover. You can edit a journal to show text in various styles. You can also decorate a journal with page dividers, smileys, and other graphics by importing them into iPhoto from your Mac or PC and adding them to a journal by hand. Some of the built-in extra content — calendar, weather, maps, and so on — reads and uses information from the last photo you add.

Design a Journal

Journals include a full set of page layout options. You can change the size of a photo or any other element, change the position, create multiple pages, and move content between pages. You can also select one of a small number of fixed background colors and textures. The design options are simple but powerful. You can easily create a layout that displays your photos in an attractive way.

View a Journal

Journals are the only way to view photos full screen in iPhoto. When you tap a photo in a journal, iPhoto hides the toolbars and other content and scales the photo so it fills as much of the screen as possible. You can then drag left or right to view the other photos in the journal. Unfortunately, you cannot zoom photos.

Create a Slide Show

You can convert a journal into a slide show with a couple of taps. The slide show option is exactly the same as the slide show feature introduced in the previous chapter. Only photos are displayed. Extra items — text, maps, and so on — are ignored.

Share a Journal to iCloud

You can share a journal to iCloud and to a "Home Page." In fact, both options create a new web page on iCloud, but the first option displays a single journal, whereas the Home Page displays a collection arranged on a glass shelf. Viewers can click on any journal on the "shelf" to view it. You

can view the journals in any web browser. You can also share the link by copying and pasting it into an e-mail or some other document. Sharing is a simple process, but it is not quick. iCloud can take a good few moments to set up and display your journals.

Share a Journal to iTunes

You can share a journal to iTunes, creating a folder with web pages that you can copy using the File Sharing option in iTunes and view in Safari. The pages look and work like a journal. You can upload them to a private web server to share your journal online without uploading it to iCloud.

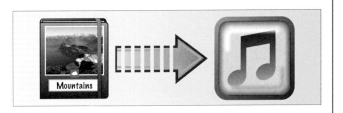

Create a New Journal

To create a new journal, select one or more photos, tap the **Share** icon, and select the **Journal** icon. iPhoto asks you which photos you want to include.

Select **Journal** and then **New**, select a journal background, type a name, and tap the **Create Journal** button. iPhoto adds the photos to a new journal. You can then edit the layout and add further content, or create another journal.

Create a New Journal

1 Select an album, event, or the photos list to open the thumbnail browser.

2 Select one or more photos to add to the journal.

Note: For more information about selecting photos, see Chapter 4.

Note: If you select an edited photo, iPhoto automatically adds the edited version to the journal.

3 Tap the **Share** icon ( ).

4 Tap the **Journal** icon.

iPhoto displays a popover with photo selection options.

5 Tap one of the selection options.

Note: Selected chooses the photos you selected in step **2**, and Flagged chooses all flagged photos.

Note: iPhoto limits the number of photos you can add. Grayed out features like the All option here are over the limit.

Note: You can use the Choose option to view the thumbnails again and select further photos.

6 Tap the name field.

iPhoto displays the keyboard, or enables input from an external Bluetooth keyboard if you are using one.

7 Type a name for the new journal.

Note: You cannot change the name that appears on the Journals page after you create it.

8 Tap one of the preset styles for the journal to select it.

9 Tap the **Create Journal** button.

Note: You can tap the **Back** button at the top of the popover to go back to a previous step.

10 Tap the **Done** button to continue viewing and editing photos or if you want to add further photos to the journal.

Ⓐ You can tap the **Show** button to close the editor and thumbnail view and open the journal.

Change a Journal's Background

Journals offer six preset backgrounds and layouts. The default is Cotton, which displays photos on a light fabric. Border is identical, but adds a thin white border around each photo. Denim is a dark gray fabric. Light and Dark are plain near-white and near-black colored backgrounds. Mosaic is similar to Dark but leaves no spaces between photos.

You can change the background at any time by tapping the settings (gear) icon and selecting one of the backgrounds in the popover. To preview a different background, tap the thumbnail in the popover.

Change a Journal's Background

1 If your journal is not already open, tap the **Journals** button.

2 Tap the journal to open it.

A iPhoto displays the contents of the journal.

3 Tap the **Edit** button to enable editing.

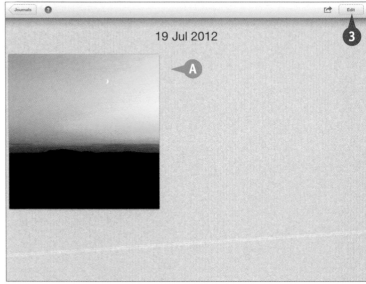

④ Tap the settings (gear) icon (✦).

iPhoto displays a popover with a preview of the different backgrounds.

⑤ Tap one of the thumbnails to select a different background.

Note: iPhoto updates the background at each selection.

Note: You can tap anywhere outside the popover to hide it.

Note: iPhoto also displays the background selection popover when you create a new journal or add photos to an existing journal.

TIPS

Can I create my own backgrounds?
It would certainly be useful to add custom colors and textures, but this option is not available in the current version of iPhoto. It may perhaps be added later. For now the backgrounds are fixed, and you cannot customize them.

Why does the Mosaic background leave no space between photos?
This is a deliberate design choice. As the name suggests, the Mosaic background creates a mosaic of images. You can use it to create a custom thumbnail grid. The other backgrounds are designed to look more like printed photos on fabric or plain paper.

Add Photos to a Journal

To add one or more photos to an existing journal, repeat the steps used to create a new journal, but select an existing journal as the destination from the list that appears in the popover. Not all journals will appear in the list, so you may need to scroll down.

By default, iPhoto automatically creates a new page whenever you add photos. This is rarely what you want, especially when you add photos singly. For better results, select a page before you add the photos.

Add Photos to a Journal

1 Select an album, event, or the photos list to open the thumbnail browser.

2 Select one or more photos to add to the journal.

Note: For more information about selecting photos, see Chapter 4.

3 Tap the **Share** icon (⬆).

iPhoto displays a popover with share options.

4 Tap the **Journal** icon (see the section "Create a New Journal" for an example).

5 Tap **Selected**, **Flagged**, **All**, or **Choose Photos** to select the photos to add.

6 Tap the **Journal** button when it appears.

A iPhoto displays a list of journals.

7 Tap the name of the journal to which you want to add photos.

Note: You can drag the list up and down to scroll through it.

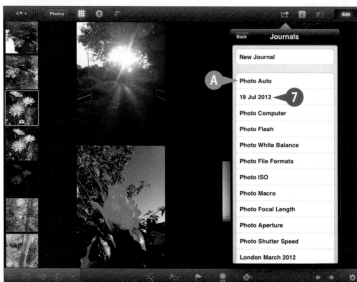

iPhoto displays a page selection popover.

8 Tap the **Page** button.

Note: If you leave Automatic selected iPhoto creates a new page in the journal for the photo or photos. Select a page manually to add the photos to it.

9 Tap one of the **Pages** options.

Note: Typically you add photos to Page 1 or another page that already exists, but you can select New Page here to create a new page for the photo.

10 Tap the **Back** button.

11 Tap the **Add to Journal** button in the previous popover to add the photos.

iPhoto adds the photos to the journal and displays a dialog asking if you want to show it, or if you are done and want to continue editing and viewing photos.

TIPS

Why do the photos have different sizes?
If you add multiple photos, iPhoto attempts to create an attractive layout. It does not "look" at the photos or try to select which photos are more important. The default layout can usually be improved with manual editing.

Does iPhoto copy captions?
If you caption a photo in the thumbnail browser and add it to a journal, iPhoto copies the caption and includes it automatically. See Chapter 6 for details.

Add Other Items to a Journal

Albums and events can only include photos. Journals can also include text in various formats, and other content including maps, weather icons, and a calendar date display.

To add other items, tap the **Edit** button, tap ✚, and select the content from a popover. The text options add text on various backgrounds. You can add a header, a plain description, a yellow stick-on note, a divider, and a "memory," a note with torn paper edges. Some content includes extra settings. For example, you can tap a Date to turn off auto-lookup and set the date manually.

Add Other Items to a Journal

1 Open a journal.

2 If Edit mode is not already selected, tap the **Edit** button.

3 Tap ✚ to add other content.

iPhoto displays a content popover with various items.

4 Tap any item to add it to the journal.

Note: This example adds a Memory item.

A iPhoto adds the item to the journal. Items with editable text display the keyboard automatically.

Note: Some items do not have a visible boundary around them.

5 For items that show text, type on the keyboard to edit the text.

6 Tap the **Hide** button when done to hide the keyboard.

iPhoto edits the item and displays your new text.

Note: You can add as many extra items to a journal as you want.

Note: You can customize items that show text (including the main heading) by tapping them and selecting border, text style, and layout options from a popover.

TIPS

Can I add video clips to a journal?
If you create a live recording with the Camera app, it appears on your device camera roll in the usual way, and you can add it to a journal. Video clips appear as stills in the journal. You can play them by tapping the play icon in the full-screen view.

How does iPhoto know the weather for a photo?
iPhoto uses the history feature at Weather Underground (www.wunderground.com) to find the weather for the date and location of the last photo you add. The photo must include location information. You can also set the weather manually by double-tapping a weather icon and turning off the **Auto** switch. If you delete a photo, you must turn Edit mode off and on again before adding a weather item. Otherwise, iPhoto does not know which photo to find details for.

Lay Out a Journal Automatically

If you have a lot of photos, notes, and other content, you can save time by using the single-tap automatic layout feature to lay out pages for you. This feature is a good way to minimize wasted space.

To use this feature, tap the **Edit** button, tap the settings (gear) icon, and tap one of the preset layout buttons. You can also set a small, medium, or large grid size. Use the layout as a starting point — you can resize and move content by hand to make the layout look even better, as described in the next section.

Lay Out a Journal Automatically

1. Open a journal.

2. If Edit mode is not already selected, tap the **Edit** button.

3. Tap the settings (gear) icon (⚙).

4. Tap one of the preset layout buttons.

Note: Use the layout thumbnails in the popover as a guide. The final layout may not match the thumbnails exactly, but it will be close.

iPhoto adjusts the layout to match the preset.

5 Tap a different thumbnail to change the layout.

iPhoto rearranges the layout again.

6 Tap one of the Grid Size buttons to change the size of the items on the layout.

iPhoto resizes the content and rearranges the layout to fit it onto the screen.

Note: The effect of the Grid Size options is most obvious if you select the grid layout thumbnail at the bottom right.

Note: You can usually improve on an automatic layout by moving and resizing items manually.

TIPS

How does the automatic layout feature work?

This feature cannot "see" photos and does not know which photos matter to you, so it attempts to make the content as large as possible on the page using the current layout as a starting point.

How can I add space to a page?

Automatic layouts often look busy. You can thin them out by adding one or more Space items from the content popover. (Tap ➕ to access the content popover.) As the name suggests, these items add empty space to a page. You can use them for finer control of a manual layout, and to add some gaps to an automatic layout. You can also add a divider element, but dividers disappear if you use the automatic layout option.

Move and Resize Items

You can customize a page layout by resizing and moving the items on the page. To move an item, tap it and hold it. You can then drag it to a new position. Other items on the page move around to make space for it. The results are always entertaining, but often unpredictable.

To resize an item, tap it and release it. iPhoto adds a blue border with corner and edge markers. Drag the markers to change the size. You can also pinch zoom/expand inside any item to change its size. iPhoto moves the other items around as you make changes.

Move and Resize Items

1. Open a journal.

2. If Edit mode is not already selected, tap the **Edit** button.

3. If the Enable Item Swapping icon (⬚) is highlighted, tap it to deselect it.

4. Tap and hold an item until its size increases slightly.

5. Drag it to a new position and release it.

Note: iPhoto rearranges the other items as you drag and displays a translucent preview of the item's new position.

6 To resize an item tap it once.

A iPhoto draws a blue border around the item.

Note: Not all items can be resized.

B iPhoto also displays optional editing popovers.

Note: Different item types display different popover options.

Note: You can tap the trash can icon (🗑) to delete an item from the journal.

7 Drag the bottom dot to change the height of an item.

8 Drag the side dot to change the width of an item.

9 Drag the corner dot to change the height and width.

10 Double-tap the caption item to caption a photo.

Note: When you resize a photo, iPhoto may crop it to the area inside the frame.

Note: You cannot scroll photos inside a frame to set the visible area.

Note: You can tap the undo icon (↩) to undo your changes.

TIPS

Can I make the layout more predictable?
There is no way to fix the position of some items while you move or resize others around them. You must resize and move items repeatedly until you create a layout you like.

Why does nothing happen when I tap?
The difference between a tap and hold and release and a plain tap and release is subtle. When iPhoto is ready to move a photo, it floats the photo and makes it slightly larger. When it is ready to resize the photo, it displays the blue border. If you tap and nothing happens, try again.

Swap Items

You can use iPhoto's Swap Items feature to swap photos and other content on the grid without modifying the layout. This is a good option to use when you create a layout you like but want to reposition some of the photos and other content in it. Swapping items helps you define the look and impact of the journal. Bigger photos make more of an impression than smaller ones.

You can swap any photo with any other, whatever the size. You can also swap text content with other text content. But you cannot swap text content with a smaller photo, and you can only swap weather and calendar icons with items that have a frame with exactly the same dimensions.

Swap Items

① Open a journal.

② If Edit mode is not already selected, tap the **Edit** button.

③ Tap the **Enable Item Swapping** icon (▣) if it is not already highlighted.

④ Tap a photo to select it, hold it, and drag it on top of another photo.

Ⓐ With Swap Items on, iPhoto locks the layout and previews the old and new position of your swapped photos on the grid.

⑤ Release the floating photo.

iPhoto swaps the two photos and resizes them if necessary.

6 Drag and hold any box with text content and hold it over a larger photo.

B iPhoto draws a blue line around the larger photo to show you can swap the items.

7 Release the text box to swap it with the photo.

8 Drag the same text box over a photo with a smaller frame.

C iPhoto draws a red frame around two items when their sizes do not allow swapping.

Release the text box to allow it to return to its original location.

TIPS

Why does swapping depend on size??
Text boxes can include a large block of text. If you swap the text into a smaller frame some of it will disappear off the bottom of the frame, creating a bad visual effect. Apple decided not to allow this. And because some items have a fixed size, you cannot swap them with larger or smaller content.

Are there any hidden editing options?
Tapping in the gaps between content displays the new content popover. You can select an item and add it to the layout as described earlier in this chapter. Depending on the layout, the item may not appear in the gap.

Edit Special Content

You can add special content — text, dates, maps, and so on — to your journal. For text, iPhoto displays a message telling you that you can double-tap the text to edit it. But some editing options remain hidden, and iPhoto does not give you clear instructions for editing other types of content.

You must be in Edit mode to edit special content. Tap an item once to display a small popover menu with a delete option. Some content offers further options in the popover. Double-tap an item to edit its contents.

Edit Special Content

1 Open a journal.

2 If Edit mode is not already selected, tap the **Edit** button.

3 Tap any text box to show a popover.

4 Tap the options to set the frame and background, the lettering style, and the *justification*, the text layout in the box.

5 To edit a weather item, double-tap it to display a popover.

6 Tap the **Auto** switch so you can select the weather by hand.

7 Tap the Weather and Temperature settings to change them.

8 Tap anywhere outside the popover to hide it and display the new weather.

9 To edit a date item, double-tap it to display a popover.

10 Tap the **Auto** switch so you can set the date manually.

11 Tap the **Date** setting to display a date scroller and set the date.

12 Tap anywhere outside the popover to hide it and display the new date.

Note: You can also double-tap a map to display scroll arrows, and then drag the map to reposition it.

13 Single-tap a map to view more options on a popover.

14 Tap **Remove Pin** to remove the default pin.

15 Tap **Place Pin** to show a further location look-up popover.

Note: You can use this extra popover to place a pin on a location after a search, or at the current location of the device.

Note: All items include a trash can icon (🗑) to remove an item from a journal.

TIPS

Why do some items show an Auto option?
When Auto is on, the weather and date items use information embedded in the last photo you add to your journal. The date item reads the date from the photo. The weather item reads the date and location and looks up the weather from a record on an online database. These features do not work without an Internet connection. If you turn off Auto, you can set the date and weather manually.

Can I modify photos in a journal?
If you single-tap a photo and select **Edit**, iPhoto displays the standard photo editor page. If you double-tap a photo iPhoto displays drag arrows. Depending on the photo layout, you can drag the content left and right or up and down inside its frame.

Share a Journal to iCloud

You can share your journals to iCloud and send friends and family web links for easy viewing. If you select **Publish to iCloud**, iPhoto creates a single web page with a single journal. If you select **Add to Home Page**, iPhoto adds the journal to a "Home Page" on iCloud which displays all your public journals.

After publishing the journal you can share it as a weblink. You can create an e-mail with an embedded link, post a link to Facebook or Twitter, send the link in a text message, or copy it for use in some other application.

Share a Journal to iCloud

1 Open a journal.

2 If Edit mode is selected, tap the **Edit** button to deselect it.

3 Tap the **Share** icon (▣).

4 Tap the **iCloud** icon.

5 Tap the **Publish to iCloud** switch to turn it on.

iPhoto displays a larger popover and begins uploading the journal.

Note: This can take a long time, even with a small journal.

Note: The share buttons remain grayed out while the journal uploads, and an "Uploading" message appears at the bottom of the popover.

Note: iPhoto adds a small iCloud logo to published journals on the main Journals page.

6 When the upload completes, tap the **Add to Home Page** switch to add the journal to your iCloud journal home page.

Note: The home page upload also takes a long time.

7 Tap the **View Journal in Safari** button to open Safari and view the journal online.

8 Tap the **Share Journal** button to open a sharing popover.

9 Tap the **Publish Changes** button to update your journal when you change it.

Note: iPhoto displays an alert exclamation mark on the Share icon when you edit a journal to remind you to publish the changes.

10 Tap the **Share** icon ().

11 Tap one of the sharing buttons to send friends and family a link to your journal.

Note: The Copy icon copies the journal link to the Clipboard. If you open a document or text editor you can paste the link into a document.

TIPS

Why does iPhoto call the journal collection a Home Page?

This is a remnant of the older MobileMe service which offered extra features. MobileMe is no longer available, so think of the "Home Page" as your public journal collection.

Why is the upload process so slow?

iPhoto and iCloud do a lot of work when they create a web page. All photos have to be resized and uploaded, and iPhoto also has to create the web page itself. This can take a long time. Expect to wait at least a few minutes — much longer if your journal has many photos.

Share a Journal to iTunes

You can share a journal to a folder which you can copy via iTunes. This sharing option works almost exactly like the iTunes sharing option introduced in the previous chapter, with the difference that the folder it creates includes extra information needed to show a journal as a web page.

After you copy the folder from iTunes, you can view the journal from your Mac or PC's hard drive in Safari. You can also upload the journal to a web server. The page iPhoto creates is mostly compatible with other browsers, so almost all web users can view it.

Share a Journal to iTunes

1 Open a journal.

2 If Edit mode is selected, tap the **Edit** button to deselect it.

3 Tap the **Share** icon (🔗).

4 Tap the **iTunes** icon.

Ⓐ iPhoto creates and saves a folder of photos embedded in a web page.

Note: It can take a few minutes for iPhoto to finish exporting the photos and web details.

5 Connect your device to your Mac and launch iTunes if it does not launch automatically.

6 Click your device in the Devices list.

7 Click **Apps**.

8 Scroll down to the File Sharing section and click **iPhoto**.

Ⓑ iPhoto displays a list of the documents iPhoto has saved, including the folder you created in steps **1** to **4**.

Note: When you save a journal, it automatically appears in this list as a named folder.

9 Drag the folder from iTunes and drop it on another folder in Finder.

10 Click individual photos to view them.

Note: iPhoto saves the original and the resized versions of all photos in the journal folder.

Ⓒ You can click the **index.html** file in the Public subfolder to open the journal in your web browser.

Can I upload the content to a web server?
If you have your own web server, you can copy all the files inside the Public folder using FTP (File Transfer Protocol) to a folder on the server. This can be a better option than using iCloud because your photos remain private, and iCloud does not need to load or process the content before it appears.

Is there any way to create a Home Page on my server?
The Save to iTunes option saves single journals. You cannot re-create the Home Page feature available on iCloud. However, you can create a separate index page using conventional web links to each journal.

CHAPTER 14

Using iPhoto on the iPhone

You can use iPhoto on an iPhone as well as on an iPad. Although the app has similar features on both devices, it is not identical. You can get more from iPhoto on the iPhone by discovering the differences and understanding how some features offer extra possibilities.

Compare Devices

iPhoto on the iPhone is very similar to iPhoto on the iPad, but there are important differences. Although the features in both versions are almost identical, the overall experience is different because the two devices have different strengths and weaknesses.

The devices have obvious hardware differences, but other differences are more subtle. You can get more from iPhoto by making the best use of its possibilities on each device.

Compare Portability

Unlike the iPad, the iPhone is a pocket device: it is easy to carry, easy to hold, and can be easy to hide. You can use it as a convenient pocket camera to snap interesting scenes almost anywhere. This spontaneity can make you more creative. You can easily get into the habit of stopping to capture interesting subjects. You are less likely to take an iPad everywhere with you, and less likely to take photos with it if you do.

Assess Camera Quality

The 8-megapixel camera in the iPhone 4S approaches the quality of a good digital compact camera. The 5-megapixel camera in the iPhone 4 is a step down in quality, but is capable of good results in good light. The camera in the 3rd and 4th generation iPads is comparable to the iPhone 4's camera but lacks some of its options, including HDR (High Dynamic Range) capture. The older iPad 2 has a relatively poor camera and produces grainy and noisy images in all but the best light.

iPhone 4S   Third-generation   iPad 2
                   iPad/iPhone 4

Using the Flash

The cameras on the iPhone 4, 4S, and 5 include a simple LED (Light Emitting Diode) flash unit. The flash has a limited range of a few yards, and is most effective on close subjects. Although less powerful than the flash of a basic digital compact camera, it is good enough for simple portraits and close-ups. The iPad camera lacks a flash. The camera works best in bright daylight. You cannot create photographic special effects such as fill-in flash.

Using a Smaller Screen

The iPhone has a much smaller screen than the iPad. iPhoto's designers have done a remarkable job of packing iPhoto's features into this smaller space. But a few features have been moved or made less obvious — for example, the Editor displays fewer thumbnails. So the app is slightly less intuitive overall.

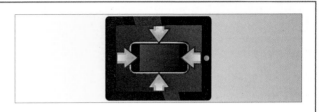

More critically, the small screen cannot reveal the fine detail visible on the iPad. Grain, noise, and other imperfections are easy to miss, even on an iPhone with a retina display. Realistically, the iPhone displays a large thumbnail preview of a photo. To get the best view of a photo, use an iPad, a TV, or an external monitor.

Using the Lock Screen

The iPhone has a useful camera feature on the lock screen. You can drag the lock icon up to reveal the Camera app, even when the phone is locked. This saves time and helps you capture fleeting photos quickly. The iPad has an animated album viewer on its lock screen. There is no quick way to unlock an iPad and take a photo.

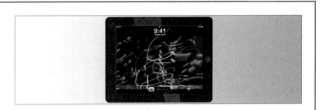

Compare Processors and Memory

iPads are designed to be faster than iPhones. iPad models also have more working memory (not to be confused with the 16GB, 32GB, or 64GB of storage for data and photos). With the extra speed of the newer A5X and A6X processors, extra memory, and improved graphics, editing and previews are noticeably faster on an iPad.

Compare Overall Ease of Use

Both devices have advantages. The iPhone has a better camera and is more portable. The iPad has a bigger screen and is better for photo viewing and editing. Having both devices is ideal. Apple's app synchronization installs a single purchase of iPhoto on both so you do not need to buy two copies.

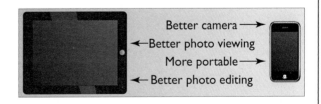

Where Wi-Fi is available, you can then use Photo Stream or photo beaming to copy new photos from an iPhone to an iPad for viewing and editing.

Using the Thumbnail Browser

You can use iPhoto on the iPhone to view albums, photos, events, and journals, just as you can on the iPad. Each opens into a smaller version of the iPhoto thumbnail browser. You can view one or two thumbnail columns, drag the thumbnails to the left or right edge of the screen, or tap a disclosure triangle to view different photo sets. There is no way to view three columns.

In portrait mode, you can view a single row of thumbnails. There is no way to view multiple rows, and the photo set disclosure triangle remains hidden.

Using the Thumbnail Browser

1 Launch iPhoto.

2 Tap any of the following buttons to open the thumbnail browser: **Albums**, **Photos**, **Events**, or **Journals**.

iPhoto opens the thumbnail browser.

3 Drag the thumbnails up and down to select a photo.

4 Tap a photo to preview it.

5 Drag the width control left or right to view one or two columns of thumbnails.

6 Drag the entire thumbnail toolbar to the right to move it to the other side of the screen.

iPhoto moves the thumbnail browser to the other edge of the screen.

Ⓐ Optionally, tap the **Back** button to exit the thumbnail browser.

7 Tap the disclosure triangle to display the thumbnail filter selector.

Note: The disclosure triangle works on either side of the screen.

iPhoto displays the filter selector.

Ⓑ Optionally, tap one of the four filter types to select it. iPhoto will display a filtered list of thumbnails.

8 Tap **Cancel** to leave the current filter unchanged.

Can I hide the thumbnails?
You can hide the thumbnails by tapping the grid of nine squares (▦), just as you can in iPhoto on the iPad. The thumbnails disappear, leaving just the main photo preview. Swipe left or right on the preview to view other photos.

Does using a retina display make a difference?
The standard- and retina-display versions of iPhoto on the iPhone are identical. The same tools and options are available, and they work the same way. The only difference is photo preview quality. With a retina display, the preview is noticeably smoother and more detailed.

Access the Edit Tools

In iPhoto on the iPhone, the edit options are partly hidden. The one-click edit icons — auto-enhance, rotate, flag, favorite, and hide — are included on the bottom toolbar. The more complex image editing options are collected on a separate slide-out toolbar.

You can slide out the image editing tools when you need them, and hide them when you have finished working. The tools themselves are identical. You can use all the tools available on the iPad version.

Access the Edit Tools

1 Launch iPhoto.

2 From one of the collections, tap any photo to open the thumbnail browser.

3 Note the one-click edit tools in the toolbar along the bottom of the window.

4 Tap the toolbox icon (📷) to view the image editing tools.

The edit tools slide out from the left and cover the one-click editing toolbar.

5 Tap any image editing tool to use it.

iPhoto displays the settings and options for the selected tool.

6 Tap the icons in the toolbar to set up and use the editing tool.

7 Tap the tool's icon when done.

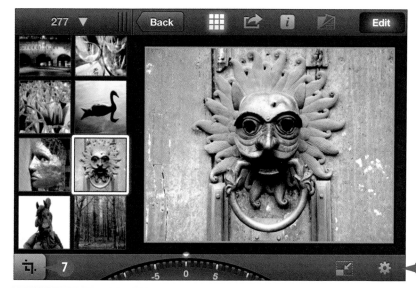

iPhoto hides the options for the tool.

8 Tap the close icon (⊗) to hide the editing tools.

Note: The brushes and effects tools display extra icons the first time you dismiss their main icons.

TIPS

Why do some tools have extra icons?
The brushes and effects include too many features for a single toolbar, so the tools have been split across two toolbars. You can access them by opening the main set of tools, and then closing them to reveal the second set. Tap the toolbox icon (▦) again to reveal the main editing toolbar.

Do the tools work the same way in portrait mode?
The exposure and color tools work differently. Their sliders do not fit into the small horizontal space in portrait mode, so they are replaced by sets of icons. Tap an icon to reveal the corresponding slider.

Using Settings and Options

iOS on the iPhone does not support popovers. Instead of displaying a floating popover for settings and options, iPhoto slides a sheet up from the bottom of the screen. To dismiss the sheet, tap **Done** at the top right.

Otherwise, the settings and options for iPhoto on the iPhone are identical to those on the iPad. The settings (gear) icons on each page display the usual features, but the layout of each sheet is slightly different.

Using Settings and Options

1 Launch iPhoto.

2 On one of the collections pages, tap the settings (gear) icon (✱).

iPhoto slides a settings sheet from the bottom of the screen.

3 Tap the **Help** button to browse the help pages.

4 Scroll down to view more settings.

5 Tap **Done** when finished.

iPhoto hides the settings sheet.

6 Open a collection and tap any photo to open the thumbnail browser.

7 Select any of the editing tools.

8 Tap the tool's settings (gear) icon (⚙).

iPhoto displays the settings and options for that tool.

9 Tap **Reset** to cancel any pending edits.

10 Tap the dot selector to view another page of options.

Note: This option is available only for the Crop tool, shown here.

11 Tap **Done** when finished to hide the sheet.

TIPS

Why are there no popovers on the iPhone?
The sliding sheets — technically *modal views* — on the iPhone were added to iOS before the iPad was released. Popovers can be almost any size, and may not fit on the iPhone's screen. So iOS on the iPhone continues to use the older technology, even though the sheets are less visually polished.

Are there any other important differences?
iPhoto on the iPhone has no help icons; help is available only in one location. You can find the Help button at the top of the main settings page, which appears when you tap the settings (gear) icon (⚙) on any of the main collections — Albums, Photos, Events, and Journals.

Take HDR Photos

Conventional cameras find it hard to capture images that combine bright light with deep shadow. HDR (High Dynamic Range) photography attempts to solve this problem by combining multiple exposures in a single image. You can use HDR to reveal shadow or sky detail that would normally be missed, such as a blue sky with clouds instead of an overexposed white area.

The HDR mode on the iPhone takes three photos at once — underexposed, overexposed, and just right. The iPhone combines the exposures automatically to create a single image with extra detail. The effect is subtle but useful.

Take HDR Photos

1 Launch the Camera app.

2 Tap the **Options** button.

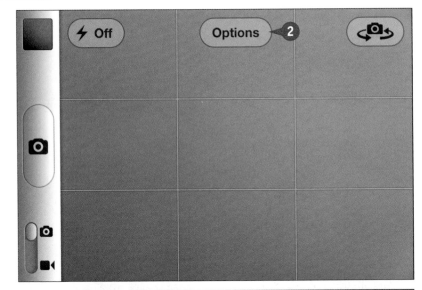

A list of camera options appears.

3 Tap the **HDR** switch to turn on HDR mode.

4 Tap **Done** to hide the options.

A iPhoto displays the HDR On message at the bottom of the screen and enables HDR mode.

5 Select any scene with bright light and deep shadow.

6 Tap the camera icon (📷) to snap the scene in the usual way.

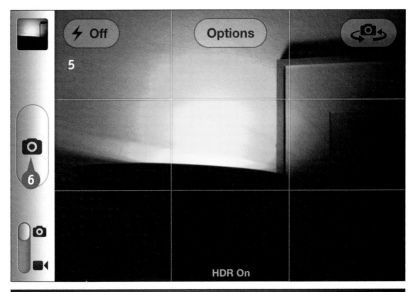

Camera takes an HDR photo of the scene.

Note: Creating an HDR photo takes a couple of seconds.

7 View the photo in the camera roll or in iPhoto.

8 Note how the HDR label appears automatically on HDR photos.

The photo has extra detail in the shadows and is less overexposed than the preview.

TIPS

Why do iPhone HDR photos look less dramatic than some other HDR photos?

Other cameras and software create HDR images by combining photos with a much wider exposure range. The results can be surreal and garish. (Brooding skies over strangely lit landscapes are very popular.) HDR on the iPhone is more subtle, and usually more useful.

Do I need to keep the camera steady for HDR?

Yes. Because HDR uses multiple exposures, camera shake can create obvious misalignments in the combined image. Take extra care to keep the iPhone steady when shooting HDR images. Use a small tripod if you have one.

Index

A

advanced effects
    adding color gradient, 210–211
    adding mood and atmosphere, 216–217
    combining effects, 209, 222–223
    creating fake miniature, 214–215
    enhancing portraits, 218–219
    gradient effect, 208
    iPhoto workflow, 209
    overview, 208
    preparing photos for framing, 220–221
    tilt-shift effect, 208
    vignettes, 212–213
AE/AF feature, Camera app, 31
AirPrint technology, 227, 236–237
albums. *See also* smart albums
    adding multiple photos to, 93
    adding photos to, 47
    All Imported, 47
    Beamed, 8, 36, 235
    colors, 9
    creating in iPhoto for Mac, 96–97
    creating with Photos app, 92–93
    Edited, 8
    Favorites, 8, 109
    Flagged, 8
    importing, 98–99
    versus journals, 13
    key photo, 90, 94–95
    My Photo Stream album, 53, 61
    organizing photos, 88
    overview, 4
    Photo Box, 9
    rearranging order, 91
    sharing, 229
    smart albums, 89
    tag, 8
    viewing, 8–9
Albums button
    iPhoto, 5, 8
    Photos app, 39
All Imported album, Photos app, 47
Aperture app, 57
Apple Camera Connection Kit. *See* Camera Connection Kit
Apple ID, 52

Apple Support Forums, 18–19
App Store
    FX Photo Studio HD app, 21
    Instagram app, 20
    Luminance app, 21
    Photoshop Express app, 20
    Photoshop Touch app, 20
    Pixlr-o-matic app, 21
    Snapseed app, 21
artistic effects, 163, 204–205
Artistic effect strip, 208
aspect ratio, 121, 131
atmosphere, adding, 216–217
Aura effect, 200–201
Auto-Enhance feature
    general discussion, 122–123
    overview, 120

B

Beamed albums, 8, 36, 235
beaming photos
    defined, 227
    overview, 105
    process for, 234–235
    speed of, 235
Black & White effect, 198–199
black-and-white photos
    adding color to, 151
    converting color photos to, 198–199
black point, exposure, 143
blue skies slider, Color tools, 149, 152
bracketing, exposure, 143
brightness
    adjusting, 146–147
    shadows and highlights, 143
brown border, albums, 9
browsing photos. *See also* Photo Browsing
    overview, 4
    using iPhoto launch screen, 5
brush effects
    artistic effects, 163
    darkening photos, 163, 178–179
    Desaturate brush, 162
    Detect Edges feature, 163, 171
    Edit Matching Areas option, 175, 184–185

Office

InDesign

Facebook

THE WAY YOU WANT TO LEARN.

HTML

Photoshop

DigitalClassroom.com

Flexible, fast, and fun, DigitalClassroom.com lets you choose when, where, and how to learn new skills. This subscription-based online learning environment is accessible anytime from your desktop, laptop, tablet, or smartphone. It's easy, efficient learning — on *your* schedule.

- Learn web design and development, Office applications, and new technologies from more than 2,500 video tutorials, e-books, and lesson files
- Master software from Adobe, Apple, and Microsoft
- Interact with other students in forums and groups led by industry pros

Learn more! Sample DigitalClassroom.com for free, now!

We're social. Connect with us!

facebook.com/digitalclassroom
@digitalclassrm